a kiwi in pang

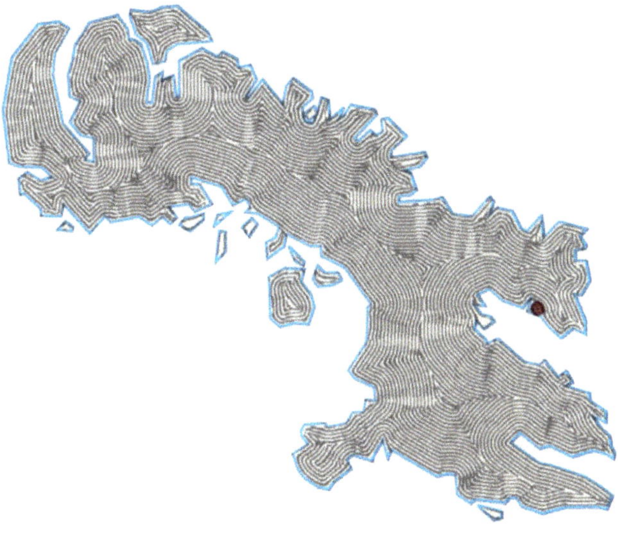

bev bevan

mmxx

Cover Photo: Bev Bevan
Cover design: Jan Kaluza

Font used on Cover and Chapter Headings: Arjowiggins Inuit (used with permission by Richard Whatley of Arjowiggins, Scotland)

Co-Published by
WordWyze Publishing
Hamilton, New Zealand
WordWyze.nz

Printed in New Zealand by YourBooks.co.nz

A catalogue record for this book is available from the National Library of New Zealand.

Paperback ISBN: 978-0-473-54379-2

CONTENTS

ᐃᓄᒃᓱᒃ

Inukshuk: traditional stone structure built by the Inuit as a landmark for travellers or an aid to caribou hunters.

Dedication

To Jean & Howard Olson,
who took this Kiwi girl in
and made her part of the family.

To Marilyn and Chuck Mears,
who used their contacts across Canada
to make my travels enjoyable.

Acknowledgements

Thank you to Peter who has encouraged me over the years
to get this book published.
I had hit a bit of a 'writer's block', when
Peter attended a promotion of a book that
Colleen had published earlier in 2020.
He realised that this service is what I needed
to get my book completed.
Thank you, PJ

To Colleen and Jan Kaluza of WordWyze Publishing,
who waved their magic wand and made this book happen,
thank you for your skills and going the extra mile.

Map of Arctic Circle with Pang shown at the red arrow

introduction: not alaska, baffin

For years, I have been introduced as, "Here is Bev, she taught Eskimos in Alaska."

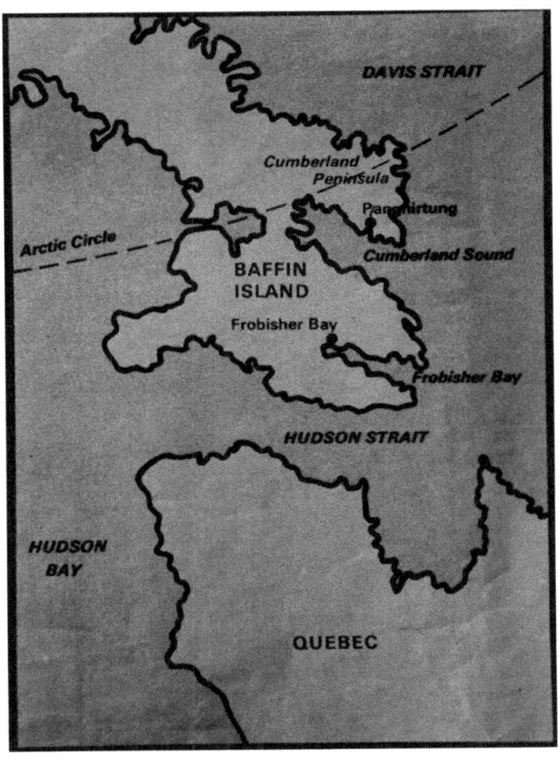

Wrong on both counts. I taught Inuit, on Baffin Island, in Canada.

Baffin Island is on the Eastern seaboard and part of Canada's Northern Territories.

Most people have only a hazy idea of Canada's North and no knowledge of the far north. Pangnirtung is situated in a fjord, off Cumberland Sound. It is a small area of flat land at the base of 4000- to 10,000-foot mountains. It is 25 miles (ca. 40 km) from the Arctic Circle.

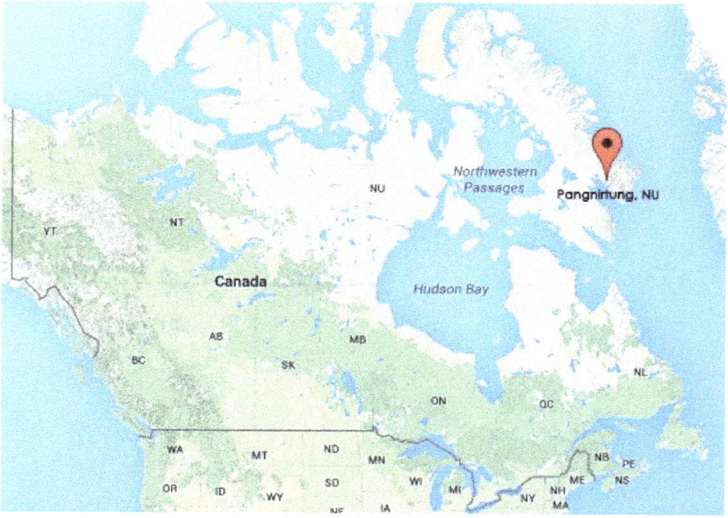

In 1967, I was appointed as one of five teachers at a school in the settlement of Pangnirtung. At this time, the people were referred to as Eskimo. Their identification numbers were prefixed with 'E', which all inhabitants were given at birth. They are now known as Inuit, their true identity.

I took up the position in August of 1967, after spending the first half of the year teaching in Vauxhall, of the Taber School Division in Southern Alberta.

It is now over 50 years since my big adventure. In 1967, when I left Vauxhall for Baffin Island, it had the same impact with friends and family as if I was going to the moon. Alaska was well-known, but the Canadian North was a vast wilderness on a map. My adventures then are still mentioned today by friends and family.

It was a time of change for the Inuit. Their lives were changing forever, and they were grappling with many new concepts, such as living in multi-roomed houses versus one-room dwellings, and new technology.

This whole experience was to be a defining time in my life.

1 the beginning

My big mouth got me into trouble... again.

It all began in November of 1966. I was 26 and had been teaching at Fairfield Primary School, in Hamilton, New Zealand, for two and a half years and was feeling restless and in need of a change.

I had often spoken about Canada and how I would like to go there. My Principal, Leo Palmer, brought a paper-cutting of an advertisement for a teacher in the Taber School Division in Alberta, Canada. Excitement gripped me; I sent a telegram applying for the position, followed up with references. Soon after, the job was mine.

I had less than six weeks to pack up my flat, get a passport, arrange clothes, and organise my finances. Canada, my thinking went, is cold… so I had lovely, warm woollen clothes made. They were to prove unnecessary, though, as all the houses were centrally heated. Friends and family rallied around and helped, and the impossible was achieved.

The passport proved to be the biggest nightmare. All business in New Zealand closed down over Christmas, and I was to fly out on December the 28th.

Christmas that year was a round of farewells. People weren't sure if I was mad, brave or downright stupid, or even if they would ever see me again.

My mother stayed home in New Plymouth when I left. We were both gulping hard, as I climbed into the car; it seemed such a long time to be away.

The rest of the family and many friends all drove up from New Plymouth for Auckland, to bid us farewell. My future sister-in-law was leaving at the same time on her way to England, on the ship Oriana, for a twelve-month holiday in England and Europe. We gave Gay a great send-off.

After much 'will it, won't it', Internal Affairs flew my passport up from Wellington to Auckland, just in time. It was handed to me at the airport, and I was much relieved!

My turn finally came, and with farewells said, I passed through Customs and walked down the long corridor at the Auckland Airport. I was really on my way.

What am I doing? I turned abruptly and walked back toward the home folks, only to realise there was actually no turning back. I was truly on my own, so again I turned… and walked toward an exhilarating, exciting two years.

My first port of call was Hawaii, where the officious Customs official gave me a good grilling. But he didn't jail me. I wandered around Honolulu for the day, and eventually flew to Seattle, arriving in the cold, darkness of northern winter. All went well until I got to Customs. I went to claim my luggage, only to find it was missing. It was all too much. Tears dripped down my face as I gazed in a hopeless fashion at the man giving me the bad news. He was aghast: "Lady, don't cry. Please, Lady, don't cry," he implored me, "I will find it."

He was as good as his word and located it in a back office. It had come on an earlier flight. Thankfully reunited with my luggage, I was now able to catch an internal flight to Vancouver and start the next stage of my journey.

I had booked a trip through the Canadian Rockies on the Canadian Pacific Railway, and I spent the day and night gazing in awe at the majestic splendour that is the Rockies. Mid-winter, the landscape was a ghostly grey-white, with trees bending under their burden of snow.

Entranced, I stayed with my nose pressed to the window, drinking in the beauty. I was unprepared for the distance one must travel in Canada to get anywhere. It seemed I had been travelling forever. Off the train in Calgary, I caught a bus to Lethbridge, Taber, and finally, Vauxhall in Alberta.

My first glimpse of the rolling pastures of the Rocky Mountain flanks, with cattle scattered here and there, gave me some idea of the farming activities. The landscape began to change again, and the flatness of the prairies, dominated by giant red silos and farmhouses, became the feature. The distances in all directions were so vast that I would become almost excited by a bend in the road.

My arrival in Vauxhall caused consternation. It appeared no one knew exactly when I would be arriving, and everyone was celebrating New Year. The School Board hadn't finalised where I was to stay. My luck was in though and, as is often the case, it was one of the busiest people in the town who came to my rescue. Jean, her husband Howard, and their five children were to be my hosts for the next seven months. What luck; Jean was a compassionate, caring lady. Howard, dashing in and out, gave me his support.

I enjoyed being part of a big family and was soon helping out with the family chores.

Jean made it her business to introduce me to all the people and activities in Vauxhall. I never turned an opportunity down, and so began one of the most exciting times in my life.

Chuck and Marilyn Mears were to become a very important part of my life. Chuck was the local RCMP (Royal Canadian Mounted Police) Sergeant, in a two-man office. They had an extensive network of friends and colleagues throughout Canada. The RCMP were posted to many different places during their service. Marilyn used this to my advantage by arranging contacts across Canada when I later travelled during the summer. Such wonderful, hospitable people.

Vauxhall was a small farming-community town centred around potato and grain growing, with ranching in the foothills. It was a vibrant little town, with a curling rink, its own rodeo, many socially active groups, and service stores for the local farming community.

Jean & Howard's home.

It was the middle of winter, and the local farmers came in most days to chat and drink a few beers while western music blared out, helping to create an enjoyable atmosphere. When I returned in the year 2000, I discovered that this once-vibrant community had suffered the same fate as many other small rural towns, with shops boarded up and an air of quiet desolation about it all. I was saddened to see so much lost.

Howard discovered I was a country girl who knew how to milk cows, so on rare occasions, I would get a phone call, "Could you milk Donkey?" (the family cow). Donkey lived in a snow-clad field down the road, and her shelter was a rather shaky, red barn that let in many breezes. I would go out in the snow and call her, and she would emerge out of the mist into the barn and eat her hay with considerable pleasure while I milked. I enjoyed her warmth as I leant against her flank; it brought good memories of home.

Curling was to become a passion. I had finally discovered a sport I could participate in, but - horror of horrors - I was expected to wear long pants! New Zealand at that time frowned on women wearing such garments, especially women of my larger portions.

I took up the challenge, however, and have worn them ever since. So much more sensible.

Two teams let this inexperienced Kiwi girl in as lead player, and I was away. I have a trophy to prove that, against all odds, we managed to win one Bonspiel. I treasure that trophy.

The single teachers, wonderful people from America and Canada, who lived in teacherages (school-houses) on the school grounds, made sure I was taken to all the important events. We would often travel 300 miles or more to attend functions. One memorable weekend, we went to the University Orientation in Edmonton. Without much sleep, but having had a lot of fun, school was a struggle on Monday.

The curiosity value of an accent can never be downplayed. I was invited everywhere and never turned an invitation down. I travelled all over Canadian West, and down into Montana into the Rocky Mountains.

At the end of summer, the whole community gathered at a local ranch for the annual branding of the calves. It was still the 'rope 'em and drag 'em bellowing to the fire' method. The hot iron put the appropriate brand on. If it was a bull calf, the testicles were carefully removed and put into a large bowl for later. The calf, bellowing and, no doubt, in considerable pain, was released to find a consoling drink from Mum.

The calves being castrated – Chuck in the red shirt

Each family had brought large amounts of food and drink for everyone to share. The 'prairie oysters' were carefully washed, dipped in egg, floured, put in breadcrumbs and then deep-fried. Many glances and snide remarks were aimed in my direction to see how I would take all this. I loaded my plate, and there, on a far edge, appeared my 'prairie oyster'. Avoiding all the looks, I eventually managed to eat it and was pleasantly surprised that it didn't taste at all bad. Relief! I had passed the test.

Castration of the calves – Howard holding the back leg.

In the midst of all this jollification, I still had to teach. I taught a delightful class of 2nd Graders. Some of my 'modern' New Zealand methods startled the School Division, but they must have approved for I was asked to stay. Summer was coming, and this meant I was free to move on. My lack of University Entrance (a New Zealand qualification), meant I couldn't teach in many provinces. This was disappointing.

I applied for a position in Pangnirtung, a remote Inuit settlement on Baffin Island. Then I proceeded to tell everyone about it with much laughter because people couldn't believe I would do anything so foolish.

Then, one morning, the phone rang at 4am.

"Miss Andrews," asked a voice.

"Yes."

"We would like to offer you the position in Pangnirtung. Could you please report to Ottawa in the middle of August for an orientation course?"

My big mouth!

An excerpt from the Waikato Times

TEACHER FOR ICY OUTPOST

A former Hamilton girl will teach in a sparsely populated land of perpetual ice and snow.

She is 26-year-old Beverley Andrews, who has accepted a position to teach Eskimo children on Baffin Island, 50 miles from the Artic Circle.

Beverley was teaching in Vauxhall in the State of Alberta.

In a letter to a friend, Mrs J. de Winter, of Hamilton, Beverley, a former teacher at Fairfield School, wrote that she had decided to take the position.

"I will be teaching at a small mission centre, called Pangirtung, 50 miles from the Arctic Circle," she said.

"It will be a wonderful experience — and a well paid one too. I will be earning $NZ5200 a year."

Beverley said she would have to attend an orientation course in Ottawa, before leaving for the outpost.

Once there she would literally have to remain in the town for 10 months.

"A supply ship visits the place only once a year," she said.

"But I think we will be in contact with the outside world by plane."

The average temperature of the area was about 20 below in winter and about 45° above during summer, said Beverley. Winds of up to 100 mph were not uncommon.

But she said that even if the weather presented a problem, food and housekeeping orders would not.

"Rations of food are issued to each person every month," she said. "I certainly won't have any trouble working out menus."

Mrs de Winter said Beverley had been in Canada for about 18 months.

She hoped to stay in that country for about three years and then travel to Europe.

MISS ANDREWS

2 summer fun

School finished in July, and I realized with great anticipation that I had two whole months to myself. By the end of that time, I hoped to have gone three parts of the way across Canada and down into the Western USA.

My farewells from Vauxhall were prolonged and sad. My host family, the Olsons, had become particularly special, and I was going to miss them terribly. Chuck and Marilyn Mears, with typical Canadian thoughtfulness, had arranged my trip across Canada, where I was passed from hand to hand and had a wonderful summer.

After the weeklong farewells from Vauxhall, I left with Diane, a fellow teacher, to go to the Calgary Stampede. On our first morning after settling in at our lodgings, we headed off. My letter home at the time details the fun we had:

> The downtown section of Calgary was closed for the morning, and Stampede had taken over. Everywhere you looked, there were cowboys and cowgirls; some were the genuine article, while others were the real pseudo. Everyone was dressed for the occasion; big backsides squeezed into tight jeans were quite a sight.

Opposite Page: Posing with the Native American Chief

Wigwams as a side display

One of the street scenes during the Calgary Stampede

We started to explore, and the first thing we saw was a Country and Western band. These were set up in all the streets, each wailing away their own brand of song. As we were watching, one band leader stopped and asked if I was from out of town. I said I was, and nothing would have it, but that I had to have my photo taken with them. Chuckwagons set up around the streets were serving breakfast of flapjacks and bacon. This was part of the service, and all added to the colour and noise. Some areas of the streets had been roped off and were all set up for square dancing - my feet were tapping. I had my photo taken with an Indian Chief in full regalia. Very exciting, but I hadn't realised that I was supposed to slip him some money for the privilege.

Mexican Band

One of my favourite bands there was the Herb Alpert and his Tijuana Band. They played rousing horns, and I purchased one of their albums.

After three hours of this, we decided to move into the Stampede grounds and see what was on offer. As soon as we arrived there, we saw food booths for the next mile, vying with each other for our custom at exorbitant prices. The Midway, or sideshows, are just out of this world; beats anything we have at home, price-wise as well. Barkers screaming, machines clicking, money going; with our budgets in mind, we managed to avoid most of them.

Throbbing feet got the better of us, so we sat on some bleachers and watched a Mexican Show put on courtesy of the Mexican Government. Singing and dancing, dressed in their own vivid ethnic costumes, they came from many different parts of Mexico. These were excellent, and I went back three times to watch them. With 30-degree temperatures and the state of our feet, we decided to call it a day.

A reviving weekend in Banff saw us back in Calgary, at 8 o'clock Monday morning to watch the parade. Even so, we had to stand in the third row. It was quite some time to wait, as the parade wasn't to start for another two hours. As the sun rose, the more unbearable became the heat. At long last, it all began. I have never been so enthralled in all my life. For two hours, we stood, as scene after scene unfolded before our eyes. First came the dignitaries; some in the latest cars and some on horses.

Each year, some famous Canadian is honoured, and this year it was Nancy Green, the skier. She was a popular choice and a most delightful person. Each year, they also had a movie or TV star from a Western series. That year it was Peter Brown from the TV series, Laredo.

There were bands placed all through the Parade, so there was a steady stream of music the whole time. Floats, Indians, cowboys, chuckwagons, this is the colour and pageantry for Stampede. By the time the Parade had finished, all the people were at fever pitch and raring to go. It was estimated 250,000 watched the parade that day, and 99,000 went through the gates at the grounds.

Tuesday, we went to the field events. These were all the standard rodeo events that had been happening throughout the West during the summer. Calgary is an important part of the round for the coveted top prize of the year.

> At one time they announced a cowboy from New Zealand as a contestant. "Yahoo" I yelled, drawing all eyes. You can imagine how I felt when that Cowboy promptly fell off his horse.
>
> Chuckwagon races, what tense excitement! These are on each night and are the highlight of the Stampede. The whole idea is that four wagons race in a figure 8 around barrels and then around the course. There are four outriders to each team. Their job is to get the wagon loaded, mount their horse and race after the wagon. Meanwhile, the wagon with a four-horse span has taken off at a great pace. The drivers have to be very skilled to drive these horses. The race is completed when the last rider for the team crosses the line. These horses are specially bred and trained; they don't waste any time. Sometimes there is a crash or two, and this adds to the fun and excitement.
>
> The fireworks displays that follow these are a fitting finale to the evening. While there, I took advantage of the shows on offer and went to see Al Hirt, trumpet player, and Rich Little, a comedian who could impersonate 200 different people within a few moments. I was later to get his autograph on my hat; hero-worship stuff. There are displays of horses, cattle, handcrafts, and anything else you can think of, is there. It takes a week to cover the whole grounds, a truly wonderful experience.

John, one of the teachers from Vauxhall, had invited me to stay with him and his family. A Vietnam veteran, John was carving out a life for himself teaching. His parents had emigrated from Europe and settled in Laurel, a small oil-refining town, in Montana. They made me feel very welcome. It was a journey of 600 miles from Lethbridge, and I decided to tackle it in one day.

Bearpaw Mountain

Northern Montana was just like Alberta, with rolling grassland prairies, as far as the eye could see. After leaving the town of Billings, the landscape began to change. I was completely entranced as I gazed at the beautiful scenery. The backdrop of the mountains, with the trees and sage, was a sight I won't forget in a hurry.

John had arranged a trip up in the mountains during the weekend, and I quote from my letter:

> John took me through many of the back roads and into the mountains towards Yellowstone Park. You climb steadily on these switchbacks to 11000 feet. All the time, the scenery is becoming more and more spectacular and wilder. As you climb, you leave the trees behind, and there above the snowline, are these tiny wildflowers; delicate and beautiful. I was filled with wonder that these tiny plants could grow here. Once among the peaks of the mountains, you could see all of these miniature lakes that appeared out of nowhere. John assured me there were fish in them. We actually saw some people fishing; they must have been freezing. We passed into the state of Wyoming while on this trip. All of my cowboy-reading days' memories came flooding back to me. This trip was one of those 'gem-

time' days in my life. John worked during the week, so I decided to make a side trip through Yellowstone Park and for the small fee of $100, I joined the Yellowstone Park Company. While I was impressed with all that I saw, I considered the thermal areas came a poor second to Rotorua in New Zealand.

Thermal area in Yellowstone National Park

The scenery and wildlife were stunning, and I was glad I had gone. John was waiting for me when I arrived back in Laurel. I was glad to see him. My stay in Montana was drawing to a close, and John had arranged one final jaunt trout-fishing up in the mountains. I bought a licence, John found some tackle, and away we went. Before we began fishing, John drove me around the countryside. Once more, I was in awe of the amazing beauty of this part of the world. Well, I tried, but all I got for my efforts was a blister, lost flies, sunburn, and to crown it all, no fish. This was to be one of the most perfect days I have spent; clear blue skies, murmuring stream, and the all-encompassing quiet.

Next morning, I packed up and left to return to Vauxhall. I was sad to leave the kindly people I had met and the wild beauty that is

Montana. Back in Vauxhall, the round of welcome-home and farewell parties started again, and in no time, I was on my way to Points East. The first stopover was to be Regina, the capital of Saskatchewan, and the training centre for the Royal Canadian Mounted Police (RCMP). Here, Chuck's parents, Mr and Mrs Mears, were to meet me.

> Regina, I will always remember for the way it rose out of the plains. As the bus sped along, as far as the eye could see, there was this flat, never-ending expanse. It had been like this for hours. To me, it seemed as if we had turned around and were going back the way we had come. It shows how easy it would be to get lost on these plains. As of old, out of the wilderness, there rose a city of noble proportions, all laid about with trees, which had all been planted by hand. Mrs Mears came to the bus station to meet me, but as neither of us had seen each other before, the inevitable happened, and we missed each other. I caught a cab, gave him the address, and was happily chatting to the neighbour when Mrs Mears arrived home. Then began an amazing visit with two wonderful people. Elderly and full of old-world charm, they did all within their power to see that I was comfortable. They had immense pride in their only child Chuck, and I was shown through the RCMP training facility where Chuck had done his training. I viewed the city by both day and night and managed to catch up on a little much-needed rest. It was with sadness that I parted from them three days later. This seemed to be the pattern of my tours: meeting and parting from folk. It can be very nerve-wracking at times.

I had planned to go to the Commonwealth Games, but a mystery bug caught up with me, brought on I suspect, by fatigue, and I decided to give Winnipeg a miss. I stayed on the bus until I came to a small town, Kenora on the Lake of the Woods. Here I booked into a hotel and for three days slept and recovered. On the third day, I decided to totter down and find the bar and see if this town had any nightlife. Here I met three guys, all local millionaires. They offered to fly me to Duluth the next day, where they had business interests. I almost swallowed it, but luckily common-sense prevailed, and I discovered they were the local police on a night out. Great story-tellers though. The further east I went, I noticed the landscape steadily changing from flat, featureless prairies to rough wooded slopes with great mounds of rocks and lakes throughout. Kenora was situated on one of these lakes. The lake had 14,000 islands with 65,000 miles of charted coastline. One day, I took a cruise to see all the overwhelming beauty.

Lake of the Woods

Ottawa was next on my list, so I caught a bus and travelled for 36 hours straight. I regretted that it was dark when we passed around Lake Superior, as the bus followed the shoreline for a long way. The scenery was changing again: the wooded slopes were giving way to rolling landscape, small farms with huge barns, and what seemed like miniature farmhouses. The severe winters meant animals had to be housed in the winter. I was thankful to arrive in Ottawa and meet Marilyn's parents, Mr and Mrs McMullen, who were to be my hosts for the next week. No sooner had I arrived than I was whisked away to Petawawa, where the family had a bach on the shores of the Ottawa river. This is a deep, brown, slow-moving expanse of water with pines right down to the water's edge, such a peaceful and tranquil place. The bach is built in the middle of the trees, and in winter, one can become snowbound, so plenty of stores are needed.

The Bach at Petewawa on the shores of the Ottawa River.

Below: Mrs Mac in the middle, on the boat

Sunday night, we returned to Ottawa for the working week. Mrs Mac and I spent the week socialising, as I prepared for the next stage - a visit to Expo 67 in Montreal.

This was the beginning of the Expo themes, which were to become a world feature for the next 20 years. On the Friday, I boarded a bus and took a two-hour trip to Montreal and discovered my school-girl French was totally inadequate in this French-speaking city. I stayed with a French-Canadian family for the week. Luckily, the wife was a Scottish lass who spoke English as well as French. Whew! Each day, I caught the Metro into the Expo and wondered how long my feet would last.

Scattered throughout the Expo site, were pavilions reflecting the themes, Man and his World, Man and the Oceans, Man and the Polar Regions, Man the Provider, etc. There was a mini rail, on which one could ride and get an overview of the whole site. I spent a week here and saw only a fraction of it.

One of the Pavilions at the Expo site

Expo 67, how can I tell you of this wonderful place in a letter? There was never a world's fair like it, and I don't think there ever will be again. Here was all the pride of Canada poured into this event, but it is especially a triumph for Montreal and the people who had the foresight and visions that have gone into this marvellous place. It's built on three Islands in the middle of the Saint Lawrence River, one of them made especially for Expo.

Yukon Dancing Girls

The theme is 'Man living side by side with his world'. Countries from all over the world were represented, except New Zealand. This caused many bitter feelings among us there—what a wasted opportunity.

Each country had on display natural and manmade beauties in many different forms. The larger countries had huge pavilions in various forms, where they vied with each other for originality of presentation and beautiful hostesses. Britain, France, USSR and Switzerland were the most popular, with queues of three hours. The USA was the only one I suffered in the queues for, the main attraction here being the giant glass dome that covered it.

Australian Pavilion

The smallest exhibitor was Mauritius, a small island in the Caribbean. They had a tent, with a most interesting display.

As well as the countries, each province of Canada had pavilions with displays showing their specialities.

Canada in 1967, celebrated its centennial with the development of its own flag, a red maple leaf on a white background, and the national anthem, 'O Canada'. National fervour and pride in their own identity were sweeping the land. The Expo was a wonderful demonstration of this.

3 Getting There

All too soon, I found it was time to go to Ottawa, find the university and venture into the unknown. My letter home tells of my feelings.

> On Sunday, 21st August, I arrived in Ottawa, and went to the University of Ottawa, where other 'new hands' had gathered for the orientation about going 'North'. Words could not describe the thoughts that were running through my head. Never before, had I gone anywhere so completely unknown. I just didn't know what to think.
>
> At nine o'clock the following morning, we met the rest of the people. It was some consolation to meet others who shared my views. We were called to order and introduced to the leaders. These were grey-beards who had seen heroic service in the North and were now enjoying the arm-chair comfort of an office.
>
> Monday did little to abate my fears, and indeed, if someone had given me $100, I would have been out of there like a shot. Thank goodness, as the week went by, things began to take some sort of perspective. I was to realise that they could only generalise and that situations varied from place to place.

Opposite page: View across the Bay

Tuesday, we all gathered to meet and greet the Deputy Minister and the Bishop of the Arctic (who I invited to tea if he should come). The course finished on the Friday after many stimulating lectures. Our group was to leave on the Monday, so we had a weekend in Ottawa at the Government's expense.

Like a prisoner going to his doom, I went out and had last treats, like a steak so big I couldn't eat it all. Little did I know that this was to be my last fresh meat for the next ten months. I made sure I had a manicure to boost my flagging spirits.

Monday, at 1 o'clock, we were to report to the Ottawa Airport for a 20-minute flight to Montreal, where we had to wait 10 hours for our flight North. As time went by, we banded together, and the time passed quite pleasantly. I decided to give everyone a treat and went and put on my slacks. It was going to be cold when we reached Frobisher Bay, and I wasn't going to suffer for anyone. We were to go by Nordair, and as they are a very thrifty company, they take you at 11 o'clock at night, so they don't have to feed you. They even ran out of water on the trip up.

At least, we were given a jet instead of an old DC 8. The journey took 4½ hours; if we had gone on the DC 8, it would have taken eight hours. There was little to do on the journey but to sleep, play cards, or booze if you had been sensible and bought some. I slept. We arrived in Frobisher just as the dawn was breaking. As we scrambled down off the plane, the icy blast hit us. We had arrived.

All the welcoming committee had on parkas and warm clothes; some of our less well-clad folk suffered. Disembarking was all rather like going through a sheep race—all these people, mostly male, stood around and eyed you up and down.

For the next hour, we sat around in the freezing air, while they unloaded the luggage. We were all cold and tired; the small children in the group had had more than enough. We went into the Federal Building, which is the universal single quarters for Frobisher. It was too early for breakfast, so we sat around and waited.

I had met the other two single girls who were going into Pangnirtung. They had taken me in hand and were busy showing me the ropes. It was here that I had my first taste of the RUMOURS that float around the North. At one time, we were going at 9 o'clock, another we were going later, or we weren't going for a week. It finally transpired that the most pressing need was to sober up the pilot. There were all the other teachers for all of the other settlements, some of them 600 miles away, were all waiting to be transported.

After all of the rumours, we finally left at 2.30pm. The plane was limited to 700 pounds, as it had floats on to land in the fjord, and they greatly increased the weight of the plane. Rae and I, being the two larger members of the party, were sent in the first flight with all of our luggage and some stores for the settlement. I have never seen a plane like it; there were four seats up front, and all the luggage was strapped as far forward as possible, to keep the weight forward when landing.

I was considerably concerned to see the pilot dashing his eyes and shaking his head, and I wondered if the sobering up process had been completed. To the untrained eye, it seemed as if the plane was plastered over in parts with tape to keep it together. I was sure I could see daylight through the cracks. I certainly did not feel confident about our safe arrival. We took off and headed north. By this time, we were so numb with fatigue; it just didn't matter anymore. I wasn't too tired to keep my eyes peeled out of the window to see what I could see with the naked eye from 3000 feet up.

The landscape appeared quite barren; it was hard to imagine there was life down there. I was entranced with it all; there were small lakes as far as the eye could see, set like gems in the brown of the country. These were joined in many instances by tiny streams.

It was a tremendous moment when, for the first time in eight months, I saw the ocean again, only to realise it was a totally different sea. Icebergs were floating along in jagged white majesty. My feeling of awe was complete.

Pang from the air

Pangnirtung, at last! There it was, below us, set on the only piece of flat land in the fjord. The huddle of houses was very tiny when viewed from the air, and it was with mixed feelings that I viewed my home for the next ten months. There was quite a heavy swell running; when we touched down, we rocked about and eventually came to a standstill. The planes must land in the centre of the fjord, as there is a reef running along the shore. They come for you in large canoes, and if the tide is in, you can be brought to shore, but if it isn't, you have to walk a mile to shore over the rocks. Thank goodness for slacks now, as we had to descend a very steep ladder to get into the boat. The thought of that icy water, just a few degrees above freezing, made me be very careful indeed. As we approached, there on the bank, were all the Inuit who didn't have measles, lined up to view us. Apparently, there was an epidemic raging.

We eyed each other with mutual interest. We had been told to smile, so I smiled until my jaws nearly cracked; I'm not sure if it did any good.

4 Pangnirtung

Pangnirtung is situated on Baffin Island in the Eastern Arctic of Canada. Millions of years ago, Baffin Island was cut off from Greenland by the massive heaving of the earth. The Arctic Circle cuts through the middle of the island; Pangnirtung is only 25 miles south of this. It is a land of mountains, icefields, fjords, and glaciers.

Above: View of settlement from the air.

Opposite page: A handmade doll

It is a land of terrible beauty and demands respect at all times. Summer temperatures rarely reach above 10° Celsius, while winter weather could send the temperature plummeting to 44 below, with the wind-chill factor. In the 1960s, the land was permanently frozen. For the brief three months of summer, all plants grow, flower and produce their fruits. They may be fully grown and only be 6 inches in height. There are no plants of great height in the Eastern Arctic.

Inuit have lived in harmony with nature here for over 5,000 years, utilising the animals and sea creatures that live here. Lemmings are the bottom of the land food chain and provide food for the Arctic fox and snowy owl. All these creatures change their coats to suit the season. All, in winter, are white. In summer, they have coats of reddish-brown to grey to suit the colours of the terrain. The polar bear lives on the ice floes and snowfields and is a dangerous and unpredictable animal. They are hunted with caution, if at all. While I was there, each settlement was allocated one or maybe two bears. Birdlife abounds in the spring and summer, with 80 different species of bird which migrate there to nest.

Another view of the settlement with the government houses.

The caribou live in small herds and forage on the tundra for mosses and lichens; they have sharp-edged spreading hooves, which give them traction on the ice and enable them to move freely on the spongy tundra. Their coats have two layers, a short thick inner layer, and an outer layer of long hollow hairs. This insulates them and gives them buoyancy, which enables them to cross large expanses of water. It is necessary for them to move about looking for food among the large inland lakes that form when the thaw sets in. Caribou provided the ancient Inuit with food, clothing, and housing. Skins were used as clothes, blankets, tents, and sewing material. Musical instruments and eating utensils were made from various parts of the animal; not one piece was wasted. The antlers were used as runners on the sleds.

The creatures of the sea are important food sources: ring seals, walrus, and whales.

The seals, in particular, are there all year round and are an important food source. Their skins provide tents and boats; the blubber was used in the *kudli* for light and warmth in days gone by. *Kamiks* were made from seal skin, with a specific pattern for males and females; to achieve the white contrast, the skin was soaked in urine. A new pair of *kamiks* was unmistakable. The long-horned narwhal, beluga, and bowhead whales inhabit these waters. I always knew when a whale had been caught—raw blubber was brought to school in the form of a natural chewing gum, called *muktuk*. The whale had provided the basis for a thriving whaling industry in the early 1900s.

Mel McPhee, an RCMP officer, who had been stationed in Pangnirtung in 1965, sent me an interesting resumé of the life there:

> "Pang is one of the prettiest settlements in the Eastern Arctic, being situated 7 miles in from the mouth of the fjord that extends many miles into very high towering mountains, that occasionally exceed 10,000 feet. It is a jutting piece of land that is grassy in some parts, especially where the Police Station is. There were about 300 Inuit people in the settlement when we were there, and another 500 in the general area or so, living in

> camps as far as 200 miles or so distant. *(By 1967, most of the people in camps had moved into the settlement, and the government sent construction crews up North to build new houses over the summer.)* Pang is about 200 air miles due North of Frobisher Bay (renamed Jqualit), and not really isolated compared to the other northern communities."

I now had a vague idea about life in the North, but I cannot say I was reassured.

5 the settlement

In the mid-1920s, the first European settlements were established in Pangnirtung. The Hudson Bay Company, a Mission Station, and the Royal Canadian Mounted Police (RCMP) established posts here. For the previous 4000 years, Inuit had lived, successfully, around Cumberland Sound in small hunting camps. Contact with the whalers hunting whales in Cumberland Sound in the mid-20th century revealed they were aware of useful goods such as pots, pans, knives, guns and duffel, which could make their lives easier. Tea, sugar and flour were added to their basic diet of meat. The introduction of the Hudson Bay Trading Post provided them with access to these commodities through trading their animal pelts, seal skins, arctic fox, and the occasional polar bear. Their basic life did not change much; they still lived in small camps and hunted as they always had, but the contact with Europeans also brought illnesses they had not had before, such as TB (tuberculosis), measles and influenza.

The missionaries introduced religion to the areas. The Catholics and Anglicans vied for souls depending on who arrived in the settlements first. In Pangnirtung, when I first arrived, there was an English missionary family with five sons, who all spoke Inuit and English. Unfortunately, I was unable to get to know them, as they left before freeze-up.

Opposite Page: View of the settlement with a tent in front

Betty down town.

An Anglican mission hospital had been established, which was staffed by mission nurses from the United Kingdom, who came to the settlement on two-year missions. They dealt with epidemics of measles, mumps, influenza, and other general ailments. The nursing was challenging and practical, with no access to larger hospitals or doctors during the ice freeze-up or break-up. Their workload was huge; they had to be nurses, cleaners, cooks, as well as be responsible for the general running of their hospital. They had to deal with any emergency that occurred. These wonderful women served the community and their Lord with great devotion.

The RCMP were important in the overall administration of the area, being Dog Officer, Postmaster, Game Warden, Registrar, Customs and Excise Officer, Assistant Fire Marshal and Commissioner for Oaths.

There were two resident officers in Pangnirtung in 1967, and they were kept busy. As well as their houses, they had a distinctive office and kept office hours, except when the mail came in. This was dealt with instantly, or the white population would have lynched them.

They often went on patrol to the outlying camps to ensure all was as it should be, now travelling on Ski-Doos, instead of using the dog teams. The dog teams had been discontinued the previous year. I was sorry about this, as the RCMP had kept their teams well maintained.

R.C.M.P. up North.

As a means of identification, all Inuit and Indian babies were given a number at birth, prefixed with I for Indian and E for Eskimo (at this time the word Eskimo, meaning 'raw meat-eaters', was used as identification). All people knew their number as well as their name; they were expected to always use their number when identifying themselves.

In the 1950s, the North became a political 'hot potato' and the government of the day decided to pour money into the area. If the Inuit were to compete with other Canadians, they would have to be able to speak and write English. Very few of the people could do this, so it was decided to establish schools in strategic places.

Woman preparing a stretched sealskin

> Until this time, they had left the administration and welfare of the Far North to the Mounted Police, its economy to the Hudson Bay Company, education and health to the Church." (*quote from Chris Bonnington, Weekend Telegraph 1967*)

The school opened in 1960 in Pangnirtung, and by 1967 there were five teachers and over 100 pupils. There were many problems attached to the programme: the adult Inuit in the settlement had very little command of English, and even those who had been at school for five years, had only a basic knowledge. The traders all spoke Inuit or a pidgin variety, and with Inuit spoken at home, there was not a heavy exposure to the English language at this time.

ADMINISTRATOR

Each settlement had a government administrator who oversaw the whole settlement. When I arrived, the current ones were Red and Lena with their children. As it is in the North, they left in the new year and George, a single guy, came in.

DEVELOPMENT OFFICER

The development officer was there to look at the possibility of work, especially if he had to go out on a hunt. We were to have three officers during my time there, such is the transient nature of the North.

The Inuit began to see advantages of living in the settlement and moved in from the hunting camps. In 1967, some were still living in tents on the outskirts of the housing area, awaiting government housing. In 1966, the government had begun a summer programme to build two- and three-bedroomed prefabricated houses and these were rented to the families depending on the number of family members. Construction workers from the south were flown in to construct these buildings. In their prefabricated form, they had been shipped into the settlement during the summer. The construction was a challenge; the ground was permanently frozen, and there were howling gales. They succeeded, and none were lost while I was there. To hold poles in, they used half tanks filled with stones with the poles in the middle. This seemed to solve the problem.

Until that time, Inuit families had been used to all living in one room, so these partitioned rooms did not mean anything to them, and they continued to use just one room. To help the families utilise the space, Betty, a compassionate, quiet person, ideal for the job, was hired. She moved among the families and showed them how to use their houses.

The popular belief was that 'Eskimos lived in igloos'. But this had not been the case for many years, although they were still the preferred shelter when out hunting and an overnighter was needed. Built in a spiral, they require a special type of snow, and a snow-cutting machete was always carried. Tents were the preferred permanent form of housing. The recent arrivals from the camps

erected their tents. These were skin structures of two layers, with moss between the layers for insulation. The inside was papered with pictures from magazines to give added warmth and insulation.

The sleeping platform was along one wall, and a small modern oil cooker provided warmth as well as cooking the family food. These people relied on hunting to sustain them.

Kilabuk in front of his completed icehouse

Lack of employment was a major problem, and many of the people moving into the settlement began to rely on welfare for a living, and the children began to lose the old skills. Some of the adults obtained employment with the Hudson Bay Company or the school. The men carved whalebone, caribou antler, or ivory from the walrus teeth to sell or trade, to add to their income.

Carving out of black whalebone

Some of these were exceptionally skilled in the art of carving, while others were still learning.

Below: Carving of a legend story out of caribou antler

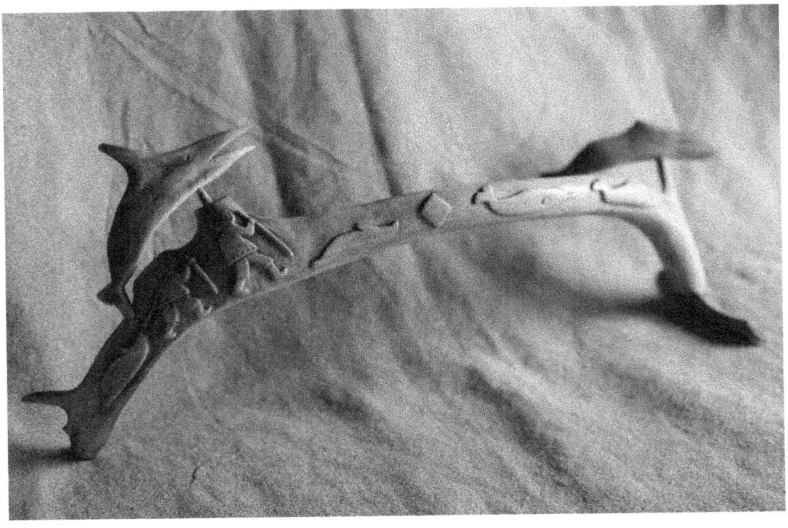

The women were skilled in needlework, having made the family clothes from animal skins for thousands of years. The caribou provided thread, needles and skin—all were utilised. With the introduction of duffle and coloured wools, their creative skills knew no bounds, and they made colourful, useful garments.

Above: Bev's Mukluks

Below: on the right, an Ulu, and on the left, other carvings used as toggles on parkas.

THE HUDSON BAY COMPANY was established to trade with the Indian and Inuit people of the Canadian North. For many years, Scotland sent brave, doughty men to run these posts. Young boys aged 16 or 17 were sent out to be assistants to the trader; they had to cope with harsh environments, new languages, and none of the comforts of home. John and Neil, both under 20, were the two lads at Pang while I was there, and I enjoyed their company.

Hudson Bay Company

In Pangnirtung, the white-painted store, with its distinctive red trims, was situated near the shore of the fjord. Each year, when the ice was gone, the supply ship would arrive with the year's trading goods. This was a major event on the calendar.

The ship's arrival was greeted in style, with old Kilabuk dressed in his best Hudson Bay outfit, firing off the cannon to welcome it in. Kilabuk had been a Hudson Bay employee for some time and took his duties very seriously. The cannon-firing was the highlight of his year.

Kilabuk firing his cannon

The whole settlement took part in the unloading, with the perishables such as flour and sugar being carted quickly undercover. The Arctic weather, ever unreliable, could change in a flash. Once the perishables were undercover, the boxes could be brought up at a more leisurely pace. The pelts and hides, graded and tied together, were sent out to the ship. No time was wasted as the ship had other settlements to visit. There is only a short window of time before the sea starts to freeze again, so supplies and annual visits had to be completed in a three- to four-month time-frame. Inside the store, was one large room with two counters running along each side, and merchandise was spread along the shelves. Foodstuff, sewing materials, duffel, trapping goods, cooking utensils were all on display. Rooms to the side and back acted as storerooms for the trade goods, and storage areas for the traded pelts and skins. In winter, a central oil-filled stove kept the place warm and added to the odours that filled the shop.

The managers of the post kept strict accounts. I was able to trade directly with the Inuit. I would be sitting at home in the lounge when I would hear a cough—someone had arrived with an object they had made. With many smiles and gestures, we would begin to haggle. Eventually, a price would be agreed on, I would write a note to the

Hudson Bay Company, and the amount would be debited to my account. Some months, my account was quite large.

During the thaw, other supply ships would make a hurried visit to the settlement. Although each arrival was greeted with enthusiasm, none was as important as the Bay supply ship. The general supply ship for the settlement brought in the year's supply of goods for the school, hospital, ordered foodstuffs from the previous year for the white personnel, and anything else the settlement had ordered. The hospital ship made its way from settlement to settlement, with doctors and dentists aboard.

This was a chance for the mission nurses to refer any puzzling cases they had, and for the residents to get their own health check. There was a helicopter aboard to ferry the people going to the ship. I managed to develop a toothache that needed attention. I had my helicopter ride and discovered to my consternation that my tooth had a hole. I was exhilarated by the helicopter ride, though.

ROSS'S PLACE

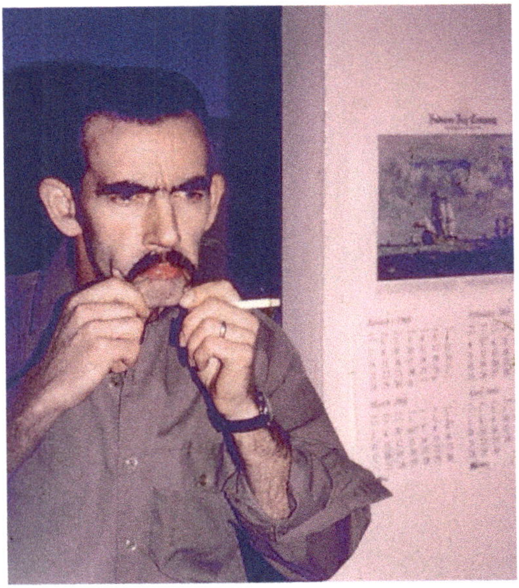

Ross Peyton was a colourful character who had set up an independent trading shop in Pangnirtung. He had been a Hudson Bay trading manager and had left them so he could become independent. He traded goods and especially carvings. His building was a social hub, especially for the Friday night dances. Mary Alice played a button accordion, and everyone learnt dances from Nova Scotia. The dances had been brought over by the first immigrants from Britain in the 1600s. It was fun. Ross had been so long in the North he could not live in the south. Like many others, he was now 'bushed'.

Caribou Stew

2 lbs. caribou
3 potatoes
2 carrots
1 onion
Water

Cut the caribou and washed vegetables into small pieces. Put in a pot and cover with water. Cook for 1½ to 2 hours. Season with salt and pepper to taste and thicken gravy with flour if desired. Serves four.

A traditional recipe in English and in Inuit Syllabic Script

ᑑᒃᑐᒥᓂᖅ ᐃᓚᓯᒪᑦᑐᓂ

2 ᐸᐅᓐᔅ ᑑᒃᑐᒥᓂᖕ
ᐱᖓᓱᑦ ᐸᑏᑦ
ᒪᖀᒃ ᑭᐅᕋᑦᔅ (ᐅᖃᓕᕐᒧᑦ ᓂᖀᑦ)
ᐊᑕᐅᓯᖅ ᐃᑎᐅᔭᖅ
ᐃᒥᖅ

ᐃᕿᖅᓯᒪᔪᑦ ᓄᓇᖏᓃᑦ ᓯᖅᑲᓕᑭᐊᕈᖅᑎᑦᑐᒥᑦ ᑑᒃᑐᒥᓂᕐᓗ. ᐃᒪᖅᑲᕐᓗᒍ ᐅᒃᑯᓯᒃ ᒪᑐᐊᖅᓯᒪᓗᓂ ᐆᒥᐊᓕᒃ ᐃᑲᕐᖏᓕᒫᖑᑦᓗᐊᖏᒃ ᐅᐸᔫᓃᑦ ᐃᑲᕐᖏᒃ ᒪᖀᓂᒃ. ᑕᕆᐅᖏᒃ ᐸᐸᒥᓗ ᐃᓚᓕᖏᓕ ᑲᔪᖓᓗ ᐃᓚᓯᕕᒥᓗᒍ ᐸᓚᐅᓛᓕᕈᒪᒍᕕᐅᒃ. ᑎᓴᒪᓄᑦ ᓈᒻᒪᖅᑐᖅ.

6 my house

When we first arrived in Pang in August of 1967, we were picked up from the shore in a vehicle that resembled a tank, and taken to Tony Patten's for supper. We were very grateful for this because none of us was sorted as far as food went. Our unexpected arrival had put the administration staff in a spin; our houses weren't ready. Tired, bewildered, and extremely apprehensive, we waited for something to happen. It was decided that Rae would have the bottom house, which was furnished. She was to have her first guest—me. We fell into bed, glad to stop moving at last. Next morning, after a breakfast of buns and coffee, I was ready to tackle the day. When I mentioned to people that I would be staying in the old hostel, a vaguely worried expression would appear on their faces, but I needn't have worried. Fred, a construction worker, had spent the summer renovating it and making it all very comfortable.

Red Petersen, the administrator of the settlement, arrived to conduct me up the hill to an oblong box on piles that was to be mine for the next school year. As the first house in the settlement, it had a breath-taking view up the fjord to the mountains beyond. It was autumn, with a steely blue feel to the air and cold enough for me to be wearing my warmest coat. I began to realise that even in summer, the air was close to freezing.

"This house catches the wind," Red informed me cheerfully. I was later to realise what he meant when 90-mile-an-hour winds rocked the house on its piles and shrieked like a banshee around me.

Red opened the door and ushered me into the dining room. I stared aghast. Furniture, still in their cartons, stood in a haphazard fashion around the room with cartons of food stacked against one wall. The overall feel was one of dirt and disorder. Fred had not quite finished his conversion, and the previous occupants had not been house-proud. I realised I would have to clean the whole house on hands and knees with a scrubbing brush, before unpacking and arranging furniture. Red took me on a tour of the house, an oblong box with a central passage and doors opening off. The first room was a lounge which looked out to the settlement. At the end of the passage opening, left and right, were two bedrooms. All of these were bare and in need of a good clean. The bathroom had a bath, basin and loo. The loo was a tin bucket with a plastic container and a wooden seat. The bag, I discovered, was collected weekly, put on an ice floe and left to go out to sea in the spring break-up (some seal was in for a big surprise). The kitchen was small and warm. An oil stove hummed away cheerfully and was never to go out.

In this small room, I was to cook and do all my washing; food and clothes all in the sink—very hygienic. Initially, all washing was done by hand, wrung out and hung on a rope pulley in front of the stove. The bonus was that I never had to wash the floor — heavy sheets retain a lot of water, and the steam created from the heat helped in the dry atmosphere.

A washing machine and drier were supposed to be on my list. The washing machine never appeared, but in October, a drier did.

I breathed a sigh of relief, no more dodging puddles on the kitchen floor.

Next door to the kitchen, was a large pantry with many shelves, and on to these, I had to stack a year's supply of tinned food - our rations. These had been ordered the year before, often with sur-

Food assured for whole year

Miss Beverley Andrews, formerly of Hamilton, knows where her food will come from for the next 10 months. She has been given the whole supply, all at once.

A former Hamilton school teacher, Miss Andrews is teaching Eskimo children in Pangnirtung, a small settlement on a fiord off Cumberland Sound, Baffin Island in the Arctic Circle. She has been given all her supplies for the whole time she will be there, due to the transport difficulties in the winter.

In a letter to a friend, Mrs J. de Winter, of Anglesea Street, Hamilton, Miss Andrews tells of the village and the children she teaches.

Pangnirtung is very beautiful, according to Miss Andrews. It is backed by mountains about 4000 feet high, and in some places, the mountains come right down to the fiord. There are no trees, and other vegetation is very small.

But in the autumn, when Miss Andrews arrived, there were tiny mosses, lichens and blueberries in bloom.

Miss Andrews said she has little or no social contact with the Eskimos. But she is able to communicate with her pupils, although they speak no English. "The smell of sealskin from their clothes got me at first," she said. "But now I don't even notice it."

Ski - doos and snow cruisers are rapidly replacing huskies as a form of transport in the north, Miss Andrews said. According to her, huskies are treated very badly.

"They are half starved, because they work with a greater will, knowing they will be fed at the end of it." she said.

"During the summer, they are kept on an island to fend for themselves, and often end up eating each other. It isn't safe to walk around the settlement when the dogs are loose."

Each Friday night, Miss Andrews and her colleagues go to the local "traders" for an evening of square dancing, which she says is "lots of fun."

prising results, especially if you were the new chum and hadn't actually ordered them yourself. All supplies were brought north on the supply ship which came each summer when the fjord was free of ice. The old hands had the foresight to order frozen goods, and we were well catered for with 'fresh' food. The new hands had to wait until the ice was 26 inches thick in the fjords. The ice, when thick enough, had to be graded smooth, then the Otter aeroplane could land again.

I was to find out later, that a case of lettuce was actually dearer than a case of Johnny Walker whiskey, and that eggs would last three months if one rotated them each week and didn't allow the yolk to become attached to the shell. Such was the longing for a fresh egg, that on one occasion, we nearly lynched George, a later administrator, when we went to dinner at his place. He had made a Yorkshire pudding with 12 fresh eggs he'd ordered in. We would have died for one of those fresh eggs. It was a great Yorkshire pudding, though.

But all these discoveries were yet to come.

The inspection of my new home continued. An oil furnace burping happily away in the back porch kept the house warm. When winter struck, and it was 44 below outside, I had ice 18 inches up my walls, and had to wear duffle socks all winter to keep warm. The heating was ducted through the ceiling; the installers apparently didn't know that heat rises. I had the warmest ceiling and the coldest floor in the settlement.

Inspection over, Red bid me a happy farewell and left me to it. I rolled up my sleeves and, armed with a bucket of water, cloth and brush, I set to. It took me three days of scrubbing and cleaning before I was ready to arrange my beautiful wooden Scandinavian furniture, brand new, straight out of the cartons. Table, comfortable chairs, and a beautifully grained sideboard made a cosy dining room. We were issued with a radio, but all I could receive was Radio Moscow, so I gave up on the uneven battle and enjoyed the record player I had ordered from the Sears Roebuck catalogue. Much more satisfactory. The lounge had two sofas and a small table. Each bedroom contained a bed, and a chest of draws, simple but adequate. I enjoyed the loan of this delightful furniture for the year.

Inside my house, once I'd made it more homely

Unpacking the boxes of rations was like having free rein in a grocery store. I arranged and rearranged my shelves many times before I was happy with the outcome. The rations contained everything one could possibly need for the year and came with a price tag of $35.00 deducted from our monthly salary. All items had to be checked off the master list in the Arctic Teacher's Handbook.

For example:
Vegetables:
Choice quality, canned:
  Asparagus, 12 oz tin, 7 tins
  Beets, whole, 20 oz, 9 tins
Flour, white enriched, 25 lb cotton bags, 200 pounds

There were no trays to go in my oven. For two weeks, I had to rely on other people's kindness for my bread and any other baked goods. Eventually, they arrived, and my baking career began, with varying results.

We were not permitted to buy food from the Inuit people. For what reason, I don't know, but we could trade. In time, I swapped bread for caribou and seal meat. Both were welcome changes from frozen or tinned food. The Inuit had little need for freezers as meat, thrown on the roof of the house, remained frozen for a long time. You always knew when a family had been out hunting—there was meat sitting on the roof of their house.

My floors continued to remain carpetless, and the temperatures were beginning to plummet. One wore very thick socks to counter the icy floors. Eventually, the carpets arrived, all brand new. Once installed, I became a lot warmer.

I felt very comfortable in my little house; it was to become my sanctuary when life became challenging and kept me safe during the worst snowstorms.

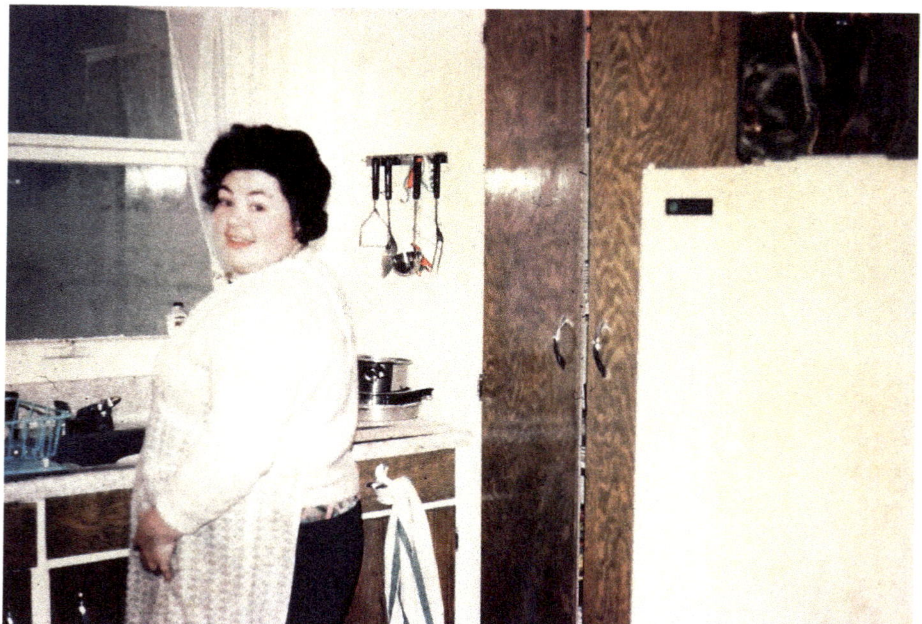

In my kitchen

7 school

The staff consisted of five teachers and the Principal. George (the Principal), Rae, Bonnie and Earl (husband and wife team), were Canadian. Joan was from Scotland, and I was from New Zealand. Rae had the juniors, I had year 2, Bonnie and Earl had the next two classes, and Joan had the seniors. My class was to have 23 students who had been at school for one year.

Back of the school as seen from my house. X is my classroom

Teaching English as a second language in Canada's North in 1967, was very experimental and stylised. There was a heavy reliance on the printed and spoken word, and there were few teaching aids like one would have nowadays. You had to be very inventive as a teacher. Exposure to English was through movies and the personnel in the village who, if they had been there a long time, had developed a type of 'pidgin English' to communicate with. School went through the grades 1-6, each class having different levels of needs as in all classrooms. Children entering school as they came in from the camps, may have had no exposure to English. Some children were faster learners, and others had difficulty with the language, as well as learning difficulties.

School was scheduled to start on the Wednesday, but the hospital ship, the C.D. HOWE, came in. George came round to let us know we had two days off school, to enable the medical people to conduct their tests. It was like manna from heaven, as we had a ton of stores to sort out and put away. Two days later, I was able to meet the children. We regarded each other with interest.

They seemed to have quite a smattering of English, and I think they understood more than they let on. If I couldn't make myself understood, there was one little bright spark in the front of the class, Peneena, who would look intently at me, give a grunt, turn around and jabber away in a very lofty manner. I suspect the translation may not have been accurate.

We settled into a routine, but I was struggling to fill my teaching time; it was very full-on with little downtime.

It was a challenge to provide variety in the teaching day. I had the brilliant idea of setting up a shop. I took a baking powder tin to school as an example of what I wanted to set up the shop. Everyone nodded. Imagine my consternation when they all turned up the next day with baking powder tins.

We eventually solved the problem, and the shop became a valuable oral language teaching tool.

Quote from a home letter:

> My last letter ended with school beginning. I hope I can give you an accurate picture of what has happened since then. I don't think I will ever have such a delightful class again. The language barrier, or should I say, the communication barrier, took 2 months to come to a workable 2-way system. They are such a lot of fun with an inbuilt sense of humour. It did not take me long to discover that the levels of learning needs are the same, regardless of creed. School proceeds along a normal pattern, with the emphasis on Oral English. It was apparent at an early stage, that the children inherit a cleverness with their hands, and turn out some of the most exquisite models and handwork. So much is in one's heritage.

The actual school building was sited near the fjord and was a single-storey oblong with the classrooms situated off a central corridor. The heating was oil-fired and was maintained at an even temperature all year. The school was cleaned and maintained by Meetook, a small bow-legged person, who sat in his tiny store cupboard, chain-smoking all day. I developed a wonderful rapport with Meetook, built on smiles, nods and jumbled language. He was lovely.

Three of the local teenage girls, Oolani, Meeka and Geela, had been to the residential school in Churchill. They had a command of English, a taste for European clothes, and were employed in strategic jobs around the settlement. Promising young people were plucked out of their environment and sent to Churchill to learn English and have advanced studies. They were returned to work in the settlement. Oolani was the school helper and translator; she was much in demand.

Getting to School

My house was situated 50 metres from the school, so normally getting to school was not a problem—out of my front door, and over to school. Early in February, we had a four-day blizzard, and temperatures reached 50 below; unheard of for around there. It started on Thursday. My house was the first in the settlement, so when the wind howled down the fjord, it shook. I was terrified. I spent most of the night looking and making sure all was well. There didn't seem to be much snow falling, but what there was, the wind was whipping up, and there were drifts all of 20 feet high. I didn't go to school on Friday. I spent a few anxious hours feeling I should be there, but I also didn't feel like tackling the whiteout conditions on my own. I was not on the telephone system at this time, so there was no guidance. Snow can be dangerous in a whiteout; you can lose your way with one step in the wrong direction. My other problem was that my house was built high off the ground. I had the experience one day, of stepping off the step and sinking up to my waist in a drift. The only way to get out was to lie down and roll on top. Most elegant.

The children, especially the girls, became frequent visitors to my house. They pored over the New Zealand Women's Weekly, my mother had sent and on occasion, went into the kitchen and made cookies—a very good learning tool.

They never knocked, but I would hear a discreet cough and know someone was there. On one memorable occasion at school, I was showing them on a globe of the world where they lived, and where I came from. Imagine my amusement when they burst into laughter and held up their fingers in a gripping fashion, indicating I must have to hold on with my hands in my land. Successfully explaining the laws of gravity was beyond me. Movies were a lifesaver, and it was a red-letter day when a shipment arrived by plane. I had asked the New Zealand Government to send me a movie about New Zealand; it duly arrived. The Principal, in a fit of pique, decided it wasn't educational and decreed I couldn't show it in school. I did show it.

School Extras

Hospital mission nurses kept a firm eye on the children's welfare. To supplement their diet, we issued the children with milk and vitamin pills, hoping to avoid the colds that float around. The showers were an important part of the week. Each class had an allotted day where lunch was hurriedly consumed, and teachers and children all arrived back at school for the weekly ritual—boys in one shower room, girls in the other. Clothes were hurriedly shed, and the children leapt and cavorted under the water, where all was thoroughly washed. The school provided towels and, after a quick dry, the same clothes were donned again. A wonderful time was had by all.

Yard Duty — 28 January

I was on yard duty, and it was 40 degrees below zero. Where else in the world would you send kids out to play in that temperature? Couldn't help thinking it was radical, but the kids didn't mind.

I saw them playing on the playground equipment in a virtual white-out. Coming in from the cold to the warmth of the school, meant runny noses were inevitable. I kept a roll of toilet paper on the table (Arctic Kleenex), so that when they came in from outside, and if the need was great, I simply pointed, noses were blown, and everyone was happy.

Children playing on a 'jungle-gym'

Joan, the Scottish teacher, left at Christmas to marry Jim, a Hudson Bay manager, who had been in the settlement. We were all very sorry to see her go. She was full of common sense and good cheer. We later heard the wedding had gone well, and they were expecting their first child. I was able to buy Joan's frozen food, which was a welcoming addition to my tinned food. Annie was Joan's replacement, and we enjoyed her company for the rest of the year.

You cannot underestimate the effect that lack of sunshine and daylight has on you. Although we were 25 kilometres below the Arctic circle, the sun actually disappeared for three months of the year. We were on a small patch of land between the fjord and the 4000-foot mountains behind us. We watched the sun climb away from the settlement in December, and then descend again in February.

February the 6th at 4pm, the sun was on my house for four minutes. So near, and yet so far. Psychologically and emotionally, we were all affected. Sadly, this slipped over into the school where relationships with the Principal and the staff deteriorated to almost open warfare. The situation never recovered, and all the teaching staff left at the end of that year.

My students and I visiting the Hudson Bay

Social Activities at School

Throughout the year, much was made of any Canadian celebrations. The year 1967 was Canada's Centennial Year, and we were busy learning the new National Anthem and enjoying the accompanying celebrations.

Adult Education

The staff were asked if one of us would take an adult education class. I volunteered—and then had many doubts.

Adult education students were given a handbook that had been prepared in 1964, which, it was stated, was experimental and subject to revision. The content was set out to inform about the area, the government, and the Northwest Territories, which were governed from Ottawa. The information presented was set out in English and beneath that, in syllabics.

One of the early missionaries had translated the Bible into syllabics. The language sounds had been given a shape. The Inuit were familiar with this version of the written language and could read it easily. The Inuit language is spoken in the back of the throat and is very visual. Facial movement conveys meaning, and you have to be alert to the slightest movement. For example, a wrinkled nose means "no". Learning English was going to be a whole new experience. The government had prepared a very stylised book in English and Syllabics. I am not sure it was a great success.

On the 12th of January, I began the class. Meetook had decided he was going to be one of my pupils. He ushered students to their seats and made sure all was as it should be. I had been keyed up for a time. When the night arrived, I was quite surprised that the ones who came seemed to enjoy it. The pupils all arrived dressed as though for a social occasion. One was late; he had stayed home to have a shave. When I arrived home, I relived the whole class again. There wasn't much sleep for me that night.

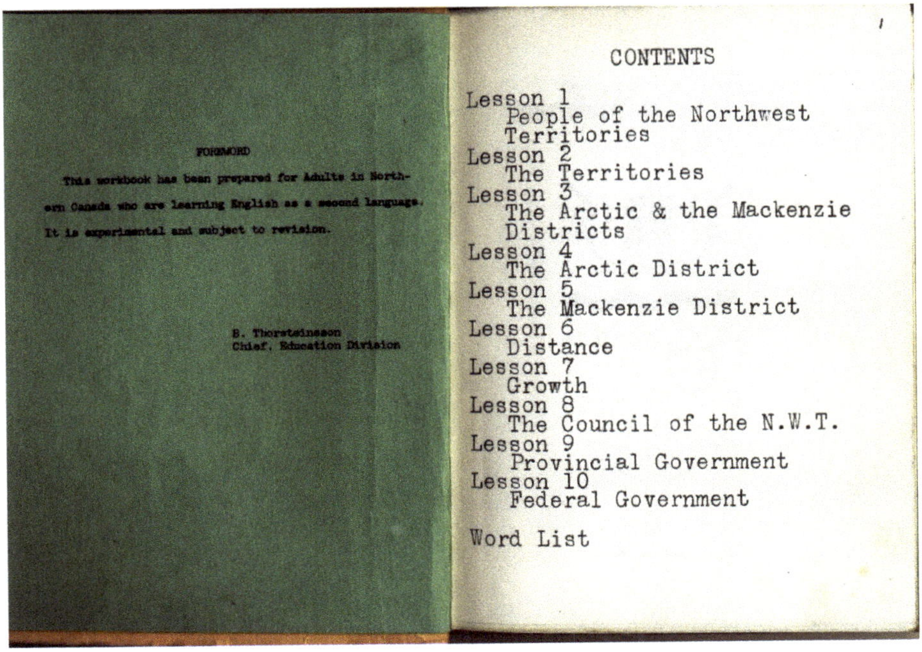

FOREWORD

This workbook has been prepared for Adults in Northern Canada who are learning English as a second language. It is experimental and subject to revision.

B. Thorsteinsson
Chief, Education Division

CONTENTS

An Example of the Adult textbook.

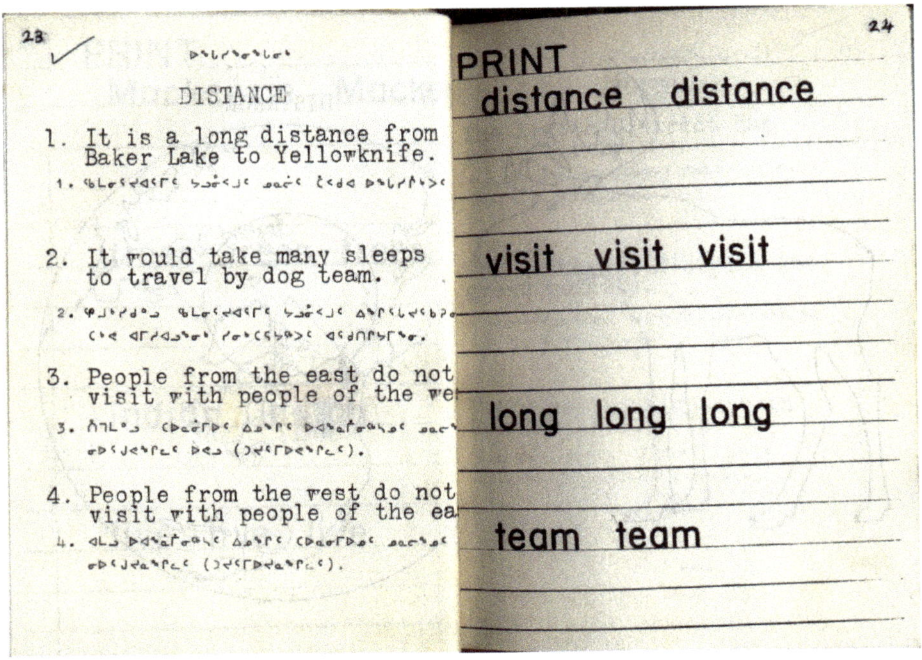

23

DISTANCE

1. It is a long distance from Baker Lake to Yellowknife.
2. It would take many sleeps to travel by dog team.
3. People from the east do not visit with people of the we
4. People from the west do not visit with people of the ea

24

PRINT
distance distance
visit visit visit
long long long
team team

18th Feb

> My night class continues at a great rate; we are all pals now. They all turned up last night and didn't want to go home.

I did have competition: when new movies arrived and clashed with my class, there were noticeable absentees. As the sun came into the settlement for longer and longer, some of the men went hunting. I was happy with that.

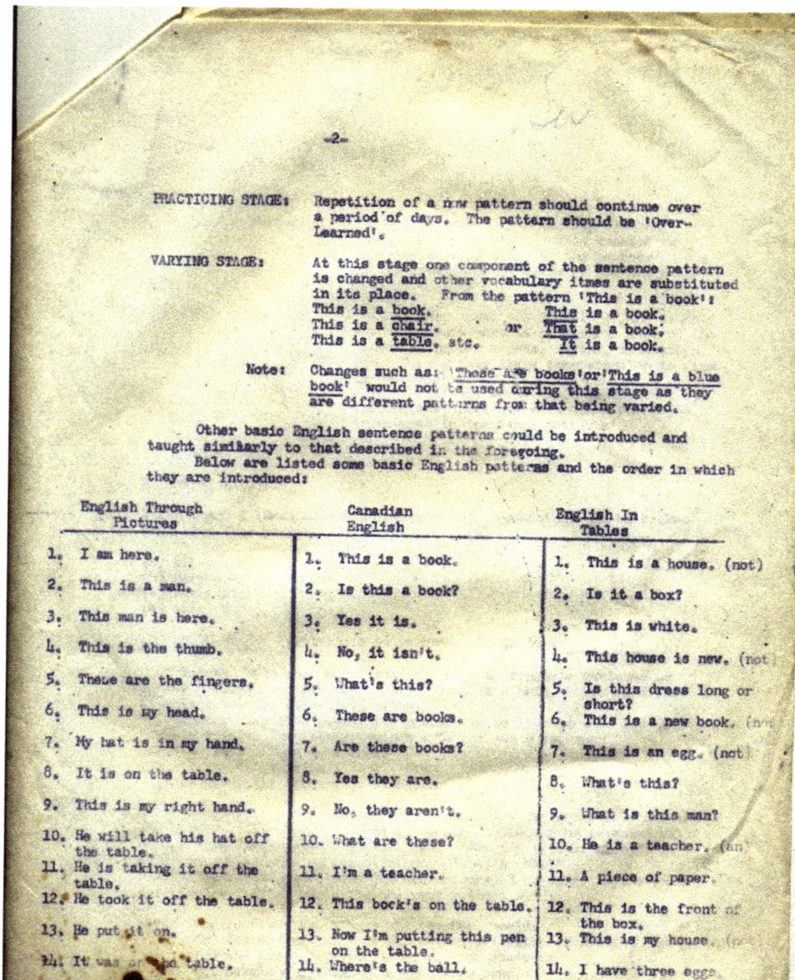

-2-

PRACTICING STAGE: Repetition of a new pattern should continue over a period of days. The pattern should be 'Over-Learned'.

VARYING STAGE: At this stage one component of the sentence pattern is changed and other vocabulary itmes are substituted in its place. From the pattern 'This is a book':
This is a book. / This is a chair. / This is a table. etc. or This is a book. / That is a book. / It is a book.

Note: Changes such as: 'These are books' or 'This is a blue book' would not be used during this stage as they are different patterns from that being varied.

Other basic English sentence patterns could be introduced and taught similarly to that described in the foregoing.
Below are listed some basic English patterns and the order in which they are introduced:

English Through Pictures	Canadian English	English In Tables
1. I am here.	1. This is a book.	1. This is a house. (not)
2. This is a man.	2. Is this a book?	2. Is it a box?
3. This man is here.	3. Yes it is.	3. This is white.
4. This is the thumb.	4. No, it isn't.	4. This house is new. (not)
5. These are the fingers.	5. What's this?	5. Is this dress long or short?
6. This is my head.	6. These are books.	6. This is a new book. [illegible]
7. My hat is in my hand.	7. Are these books?	7. This is an egg. (not)
8. It is on the table.	8. Yes they are.	8. What's this?
9. This is my right hand.	9. No, they aren't.	9. What is this man?
10. He will take his hat off the table.	10. What are these?	10. He is a teacher. [illegible]
11. He is taking it off the table.	11. I'm a teacher.	11. A piece of paper.
12. He took it off the table.	12. This book's on the table.	12. This is the front of the box.
13. He put it on.	13. Now I'm putting this pen on the table.	13. This is my house. [illegible]
14. It was on the table.	14. Where's the ball.	14. I have three eggs.

An example of the instructions for teaching English

16th March

Tonight was the last night of my formal night class. We have not worked the full course, but interest is waning. I would rather end now while I am ahead. They have decided to have a party (strictly non-alcoholic) next Monday with games and dancing.

They arrived dressed up and full of excitement. They played blindman's bluff first. Oh, the shrieks and screams, they did enjoy it. The next game had an Inuit name that translated, means 'rotten'. The idea is everyone sits in a circle, feet pointing in. One person stands rigid in the centre. They fall, and you have to push them away. It was hilarious. Inuit dancing rounded out a really good evening. I am going to miss the social contact.

Children out of school enjoying the Ski-doo

Following page: baby-sitting the younger siblings

8 Mail and Christmas

The arrival and departure of mail and rumour went hand-in-hand and was to continue the whole length of my stay there. Goods that had been ordered were equally important, especially fresh food. With no all-weather airstrip, mail and freight often had to wait till ice froze to a depth of 26 inches in the autumn, or broke up and cleared the fjord in the spring, to allow planes to land there. It was a hazardous landing at that time.

Mail was assembled in Montreal and forwarded north to Frobisher Bay, sorted into settlement groups, and sent in with whoever was coming that way. Woe betide any flight or boat that didn't bring mail if they were coming to that settlement. The RCMP was responsible for sorting and sending mail. Knowing how important it was to us, they made great efforts to get it sorted as soon as it arrived, be it night or day.

Quote from my letter:

> Talking of no mail, the lack of communication makes everything seem very unreal. We haven't had news from the outside world for 6 weeks now. History is being made, and up here, you just wouldn't know.

Planes frequently came to the settlement, either flying over and air-dropping, or landing on the very unusable airstrip. Rumours abounded about planes arriving, and when nothing eventuated, the feeling of loss was huge.

17th September

Well, we still haven't had any mail. Planes have been in and out, to take patients from the hospital, bring in casual workers for specific work. No mail.

21st September

Once again, the Northern rumours. There are two possibilities, a twin-engine Otter, or an icebreaker. Will believe it when I see it.

1st October

A twin-engine otter landed on the 'airstrip.' It isn't even a strip, and the ground hasn't even frozen enough to take planes. This plane did the nearest thing to a nosedive. We were all waiting for the crash; they had 14 people on board and NO MAIL. There were quite a few people waiting to go out, but they wouldn't take anyone. It was too dangerous. One becomes very philosophical in the North.

Sunday 8th October:

Oh, what joy! Mail this morning. A plane has arrived with mail at last. George brought it up, and when he arrived, I just cried my eyes out. Poor devil, he took off like a scalded cat. I didn't realise how much I was missing my mail. I soon recovered enough to begin. There was a whole bag filled with letters from all over, 41 in total. Even one from a little old lady I had met on a bus. Parcels and magazines completed the treasure.

The importance of freight can be demonstrated in my letter dated **17th December:**

Well, here I sit waiting for the girls to come to supper. We are having ham, salad, lettuce, cucumber, tomato. I can hardly wait. I had a huge salad last night; my poor system will wonder what's wrong with it.

We had a long wait for the next mail drop. On the 23rd of November, a plane flew over the settlement and air-dropped bags; no mail. This happened on several occasions with planes coming, but no mail. Just before Christmas a plane flew over and dropped a package. It was a Christmas tree, NO MAIL. You can imagine our frustration.

> Well, here I sit amidst my first 'white Christmas,' and I certainly have had one to remember. So many kind folks have remembered me. As you will know, air-drop was cancelled, and we had resigned ourselves to Christmas without any mail. When lo and behold, out of the blue, a Nordair sked with 2,600 lbs of mail aboard. Well, that was the start of a week that went in a dream.

Christmas Cards on my bookshelf

> I had firmly resolved that I would save all my mail and open it all on Christmas Day. Well, Bev being Bev just couldn't resist it all. Each parcel I opened, I would have a little cry. The night passed away among letters and things. I put each letter in chronological order before

opening; in that way, I could enjoy them more. Did I get beans the next day when I went to school, and they found out I had opened all the presents!

Joan was to depart sometime, but we didn't know when. Out of the blue, we learnt it was 6:30 that night. Nordair was to come in again with mail, this time carrying a measly 1000lbs. Well, by the time we had Joan adjusted, we found the mail was to be delivered. Rae came up to eat at my place, so we could hold each other up. We sat for two hours while our mail waited. Then I did it again: more parcels, more tears. This time there was even less mercy at school.

I must mention that they go in for Christmas in a big way up here. Everyone has a tree and lights, with parcels under the tree, that are left until Christmas Day. It certainly seemed more natural to have a tree with all the snow outside, not the bright sunlight we have at home.

Thursday arrived. Lo and behold another plane with more mail on it. I had promised faithfully I wouldn't open it, I didn't either. There sat all this mail from Vauxhall. I went to bed but was unable to sleep. It all became too much for me, so up I got and opened them all. They totally washed their hands of me at school.

School finished with a bang on the Friday and a movie for the kids. They were to receive their gift when they went back to the room before going home—great excitement when Santa put in an appearance at the movie. I think the highlight of all the Christmas celebrations was when the kids came back to the classroom and found the gifts which Santa had left. Their joy was a delight to behold as they yelled and shouted and literally danced for joy. It was worth all the work and the preparations.

The Saturday and Sunday before Christmas were spent doing all the last-minute preparations with many teas here and there. Rae and I were invited to Red and Lena's to watch their kids open their presents on Christmas Eve, as is the custom in Denmark. We had an enjoyable evening.

Christmas morning dawned bright and clear. I had my Christmas treat of a lie-in. I had to bestir myself, though. Betty and Rae were coming for Christmas breakfast at noon. They had ordered porridge, with bacon and eggs to follow, with all the trimmings. That was the beginning. People were in all day, and I only just managed to get ready in time to go to Bonnie and Earl's for tea. All the Hudson Bay boys were there, and we had a regular feast. We relaxed and then decided to go to the Inuit dance at the community centre.

After Christmas, mail delivery continued to be erratic, but always very welcome. As the year progressed, in order to get new clothes and other basic needs not available at the Hudson Bay Company, we had to order from the Sears Roebuck catalogue, and have our purchases freighted in. The mail delivery as it was, made this a chancy operation.

My correspondence became enormous. I was in contact with 54 people from all around the world. I resolved the problem by writing a community newsletter and posted that to most people, plus bread-and-butter letters to close family. Over 50 years later, people still talk about my letters.

9 Living in the North

In the 1960s, the community was divided into 'them' and 'us'; a situation with little or no fraternising socially between the groups. This was the social norm of the time. I never went into an Inuit house to visit, much to my regret. The barriers were coming down slowly while I was there. Betty was able to visit in the course of her work, and Anna simply chose to visit Inuit in their homes despite it being frowned upon by the 'white' population.

Many of the 'white' population were transient, touching down in their various roles and then departing again. Construction crews would come in for the summer, and then depart before the freeze-up. Important people would come in briefly on tour around the Arctic; I suspected it was a free sightseeing tour. The appointed people—like teachers, police, administrators, —were there for the length of their appointment. Some individuals became so enmeshed in the life there that they never left. Meals in each other's houses tested our cooking skills and ingenuity. If someone was lucky enough to have fresh or frozen produce, an invite to their house was much sought after. The single men in the settlement soon learnt that if they brought fresh meat or vegetables, I could be relied upon to cook them a good meal. The conversation following these meals was stimulating and interesting.

One memorable occasion, we were invited to dinner on the Hudson Bay ship when it arrived with supplies. The first night, we arrived too late and missed the tide. The next night, we made sure we were there in time. Here I was, climbing up a rope ladder from a rolling barge to a waving ship. I've done some stupid things in my life, but this was the worst. After a delightful evening and a mighty pork roast dinner, we decided we had better come back. The thought of the ladder was filling me with dread, but I need not have worried, as they had hauled the barge out of the water. Then with me sitting regally in the back, they lowered it into the water again. What gentlemen!

With autumn dusting the mountain slopes in brown and gold, I knew the children were enjoying the fruits from the various small plants that grew there—their faces were covered in blueberry juice. Fully grown plants, only inches tall, were all over the hillside. The ground was slushy; just the top layer had thawed. I joined the children one day and wondered at how the plants thrived in this harsh environment.

The first blizzard arrived on the 20th September with howling winds and drift snow. The tundra began to refreeze, and our activities were to change. It wasn't until the second week in October that softer-falling snow covered the ground.

The community was able to bring out toboggans, sacks, and anything that would slide.

Jeela and I acquired a toboggan and away we went. I must admit, I was more than a little scared; the hill is huge, and one flies down it like a bat out of hell. We were going at such a pace; I fell off once just to stop. We went over so many bumps, and I would leap about 6 feet in the air, then bang, back onto the toboggan. My bum was quite bruised; indeed, I was unable to sit down.

Mary Alice arrived with the snow cruiser, and away we went. It was marvellous fun. The weather was not only freezing; it was 10 degrees below freezing. It was time to get my winter gear. That night, I went to the Hudson Bay and spent $100, just like that.

It became obvious that I was going to need much warmer garments for outside. Annie Kilabuk was recommended. She arrived one day to check me out. With no tape measure in sight, she just looked at me, took out a piece of wool, and measured my shoulder width. A week later, she arrived with a *parka* made of duffel, and a waterproof outer layer. She had also made *kamiks*, duffle socks and mitts. Annie was a very talented seamstress and embroiderer, all done by hand. My *kamiks* were sewn with caribou sinew and made of sealskin. The initial embroidery on my *parka* was Maori in design. Later, Annie added her own design of beautiful red flowers. Local dog fur surrounded the sleeves and bottom, with wolverine around the face area of the hood. The fur was vital; in a howling gale, you could huddle into the hood to prevent your face from being frost-bitten. My hood had wolverine fur around the face and was shaped into a point, which indicated it was from the eastern Arctic. The western Arctic hood shape was rounded at the back.

Annie had decorated the duffel with colourful embroidery. The whole outfit is a treasure. *Kamiks* made of sealskin with duffel insets, completed the gear. The *Kamiks* had a white geometric pattern around the calf; for women, the pattern went up and down the *Kamik*. The sealskin was soaked in urine to obtain the white pattern. I always knew when new *Kamiks* came to school. Unfortunately, I lent mine to someone when I got home, and they were not returned.

Daily life threw up some curly problems. The following excerpts from my letters give an insight into our lives. Our arrival in the North was a signal for a 'get to know you' social round. There were no cafes to socialize in, so everyone entertained in their homes amidst much quiet competition.

There is a great transience about the North; people come in for a specific purpose. Complete that, and then they are on their way again. At this time, they were dependent on the 'break-up', where the ice breaks up and moves out to sea with the tides, and 'freeze-up' where the ice freezes to 26 inches, and planes can land on the ice. An all-weather strip completed the following year, removed some of the uncertainty about planes.

With school now started, the nurses came to delouse the kids. I asked them to check mine as a precaution. I got the all-clear. The nurses invited us down for Sunday lunch, and it was delicious with lots of fresh veggies (they had a glasshouse). We discovered it was one of the nurses' birthday celebrations. I wish we had known earlier; then we could have arranged suitable gifts.

November 5th

> Halloween is big here—a great excuse for a party. Monday, we went back to school and bagged hundreds of lollies for the kids. Then they wouldn't go round the settlement banging on houses.
>
> Tuesday, being Halloween, we had the party at school and distributed them. They were much enjoyed by all. The adults managed a 3-day party with some sore heads.
>
> My RCMP friend, Ed, received a sudden transfer and was gone; this left a hole in my life. Joan arrived with a lift-your-spirits gift box of cookies, stockings, and a book. Such a kind lady; will miss her when she goes. I must say my work level improved.
>
> Five of us gathered at Rae's for a chicken dinner. One of the guests, would you believe, was a New Zealander; she was an education officer. She had a brother, Bill Coker, a vet in Matamata. We had a good old nostalgic chat.

November 23rd

The week has flown. It's dark from 3 in the afternoon to 9 in the morning, with the result that my drapes are pulled all day. We had a regular old snow-up last night. The wind was gusting slightly, just enough to blow up huge drifts. When I opened the door, piled-up snow fell in. I had to dig my way out. The snow is sticky and slushy. Hangs onto everything, ugh. Tremendous drama—one of the rentals burned down last night. It was empty, and no one was hurt. Of course, I slept through the whole lot.

January 7th

Wednesday night, my furnace was on the blink. That can be quite frightening, so once again, no sleep. I got George over to look at it. He thought he had fixed it, but lo and behold, the next night, it was playing up again. This went on for several days until they managed to solve whatever the problem was. At 20 degrees below, it was a little uncomfortable. There were two co-op men in here. I had them over for a meal on Wednesday. It was a lot of fun to see new faces, and they were very entertaining fellows. Both of them were from Newfoundland, with the result that arguments ran high. There are quite a lot of 'newfies' here, and they are a clanny lot. The poor beggars went home to burst pipes and water all over the floor. I didn't see them again, as they were waiting for a plane out. Am not sure if they cleaned the place up before they left.

Thursday and Friday, Ray took sick, so I was running around seeing whether she was OK. Coming home one night, I heard a cracking sound. Looking up, I saw the Northern lights waving and snapping in great green waves through the sky. I stood there entranced, feeling privileged to be seeing this awesome sight.

Friday night, I thought I would go to bed early but, lo and behold, I ended going to a movie at the Larden's.

It was great to sit there in armchair comfort with a beer at my elbow. Ha, Saturday, I thought, at long last, I can have a rest... What a dream. Had to get up and go to the Post Office before it closed, then clean up the mess that I had shut my eyes to all week. Always a lengthy task cleaning up.

A plane came in, and on it they had our school consultant, a dentist, and a psychologist. At 4 o'clock this morning, the dentist was sitting in my living room, drinking coffee, and putting affairs right in Pang. Earlier, we had gone down to the dance and had a rip-roaring time. I am beyond tired. Tomorrow the week begins again.

28th January

It's Saturday again, and here I sit, just me and my shadow. Don't think I will see many today; it's 40 below outside. I have frost from the floor up the walls. I have the thermostat turned up to 80, but with the heat ducted onto the ceiling, it isn't much help. It is cold.

Ray Buffit, the Industrial Development Officer, had been out on the trail, and he called in to see me today. They had travelled 1500 miles by Ski-Doo searching

> after the white fox but didn't find any. I am not surprised, as any self-respecting fox would be long gone with the noisy Ski-Doos. They saw some caribou, though. The men all had frozen noses. I was envious of their adventure and would like to do a trip like that, but know I would not stand the conditions. Had a huge crowd on Wednesday; I had a movie which was most enjoyable. Hudson Bay George had found some frozen New Zealand lamb in a freezer that was quite badly freezer burnt. Nothing daunted, I cooked it. What a treat! Six of us tucked in before the movie. Voted delicious. My liquid refreshment has all been consumed, so Roger promised to send some in on the next plane. A case of Johnny Walker whiskey is cheaper than a case of lettuce. I'm not sure which is better for you.

February 6th

> The first finger of sunlight entered my house for a few moments. We had watched it creep across the fjord each day a little more as it rose higher in the sky. The difference is amazing. It's coming back.

My January and February letters reflect a growing desperation in our lives. Perpetual darkness affects you in strange ways. Imagined or real slights within your relationships can make for strained relations, and sometimes things can boil over in very unpleasant ways.

> Stony was the only one to come to tea Saturday. We were just finishing when there was a bang on the door.
>
> "Are the police here? Come quick!"
>
> That was the end of our evening, or should I say the beginning. There was a fight on, and some beat-up men around. I had to go and look after the children. It was 10 o'clock in the morning when I finally crawled into bed. There was one guy cut up and fighting mad. What a sight! They sat up with him all night until the situation was under control. Later, I was to witness the break-up of the home. It's the innocent that suffer, those poor kids. Nothing good came of it.

Today I was going to walk out on the ice where the sun is. It looked a little dangerous, so I came home. I managed to slip on the steps, and down I went. My tailbone hurt. I lay there and whimpered. No one was around, so I decided I had better finish climbing the steps and go inside. I recovered.

February 13th

Here it is Sunday again, and we sit out a 4-day blow. The wind was really bad on Thursday, and I spent the night looking out to see if all was well. It wasn't snowing, but the wind was whipping up loose snow into drifts of 20 feet high. I didn't go to school on Friday. I didn't feel like tackling it on my own. With white-out conditions, it is very dangerous. One step in the wrong direction and you can be lost. This happened to a father and son in another settlement in January; they lost their lives. George didn't send for me, and kids that came were sent home as soon as possible.

I was given some caribou the other day (highly illegal). It's cooking on the stove at the moment. Boy, does it smell good. I have made some bannock and have told the guests they have to eat with their fingers. I even threatened to get some snow and blueberries and make ice-cream, I don't think it will happen.

It's Saturday again, my lie-in day.

"Miss Andrews, where are you?"

Some of the kids had come to show me a new parka. There ended my lie-in. I looked out, and it was a glorious day out there, so out I went. Housework could wait. Betty and I went walking way out on the fjord and onto the pressure ice. This is water that has been frozen and thrust up into these fantastic shapes, and there are great gaping fissures. The colours vary from white to green to blue, and graunching sounds are loud in the clear air. Very awe-inspiring. Tomorrow, if the weather remains fine, we are supposed to be going across the fjord to play ice hockey. I will be side-line audience. Broom Ball is proving to be a lot of fun. It's played with the yard broom and ball, and it bears a vague resemblance to ice hockey.

Playing Broom Ball on the ice

The kids have begun coming to my house and making cookies. They have a wonderful time in the kitchen, and their English is certainly improving. New Zealand Woman's Weekly is scanned in great depth, with many giggles.

March 11th

No mail, no mail, the constant theme song. I am sending this letter out with Doug to post in Frobisher Bay when he goes for a conference. We have been having glorious weather. The sun has been streaming in, and it surely warms my house up. I have windows on all sides of the house, and it is in there all day. Friday night, I made another batch of bread but consigned it to the flames. I'm damned if I can get it right at the moment.

Saturday, I leapt out of bed at midday into some clothes, and off outside. Betty and I wandered around and had a good old walk; it was only 30 below. We ended up at the hospital and scrounged a cup of tea from the girls. By that time, we needed it—we were feeling a little chilly.

Sunday, Bonnie got me out of bed to cut my hair. Betty arrived, then George, to unfreeze some of my pipes. You would have laughed to see Bonnie and Betty cutting my hair. It took hours with snips here and there; great hilarity. At least it is shorter and tidier.

I am now the proud possessor of a PHONE, number 16. The Bell telephone company were in, and finally connected me up, only 7 months late. It has certainly created a new aspect on living. Contact with people is only as far away as the phone.

March 24th

Betty departed Thursday after a few alarms. We are going to miss her. Suddenly realised Thursday night that I was the only one up this end of the settlement. I spent the night imagining all sorts of scenarios. They tell me the new Development Officer will be in shortly. They will be just up the hill. Phew.

I have sitting on my windowsill a piece of willow in some water. I had found it on one of my walks. I hope it comes out. Yes, they are here, just about ground level, and may be a hundred years old. Amazing.

10 The Highlight: Dogsled Ride

I was very keen to go on a dogsled ride. One day, when the sun had returned, and the ice was beginning to melt, Meeka and Kilabuk said, "Today is the day."

The dogs were very badly treated, the idea being that if you didn't feed them, they would pull harder, knowing they were going to be fed at the end. My farm upbringing never came to terms with this theory. The dogs were the mainstay of any form of travel until the Ski-Doo was invented in 1959 by Bombardier in Montreal and introduced to the region in 1962. This changed the face of the North. The RCMP dogs had been retired the year before, and Ski-Doos issued. I was sorry about this, as the RCMP cared well for their dogs, and were a source of pride to their handlers.

Kilabuk had put a team together, and I was told to sit on the *komatik* (sled), which was a basic sled on runners, with skins covering the flat surface to provide you with a seat. We had a gun along. The idea was to look for a seal hole and catch a seal out. Fortunately, we didn't see a seal. I am not sure I could have shared the *komatik* with a dead seal.

The traditional *komatik* was equipped with all the equipment needed for a lengthy stay away: saws, machetes, spears, gun, and equipment for cooking. When Ski-Doos were used and broke down far away from the settlement, this became a problem. Dogs could be counted on to get you home. It was a dilemma each family had to work through.

With the dogs hitched up, away we went. At one time, I decided my cramped legs needed exercise, so I jumped off and ran. The dogs were much faster than I was. They had to pull up while I scrambled back on. Was my face red!

The ice was melting, and several of the dogs soon had bloody paws where the ice shards had cut them. The ice along the shoreline was creaking, groaning, grinding and pushing up into fantastic shapes. The rock faces behind glistened in the sun. The mountains behind that climbed into the clear blue sky. What beauty surrounded us. We were headed down toward Cumberland Sound. It wasn't long before we were out in the open sound, where the ice seemed to stretch forever. Kilabuk had his boil-up Inuit-style, and we enjoyed the sunshine and warm drink. Moving around the ice, I fell into a chasm that had opened up in the ice. Luckily it wasn't too wide, and I was able to scramble out. I was mortified. Obviously, I didn't have the Inuit eye for the 23 different varieties of snow and ice.

We soon headed home, and the dogs pulled with a will.

My dogsled ride made for a truly memorable day.

Above: The side-view of the sled we went out on.
Below: A carving of a sled and dogs, equipped for the hunt.

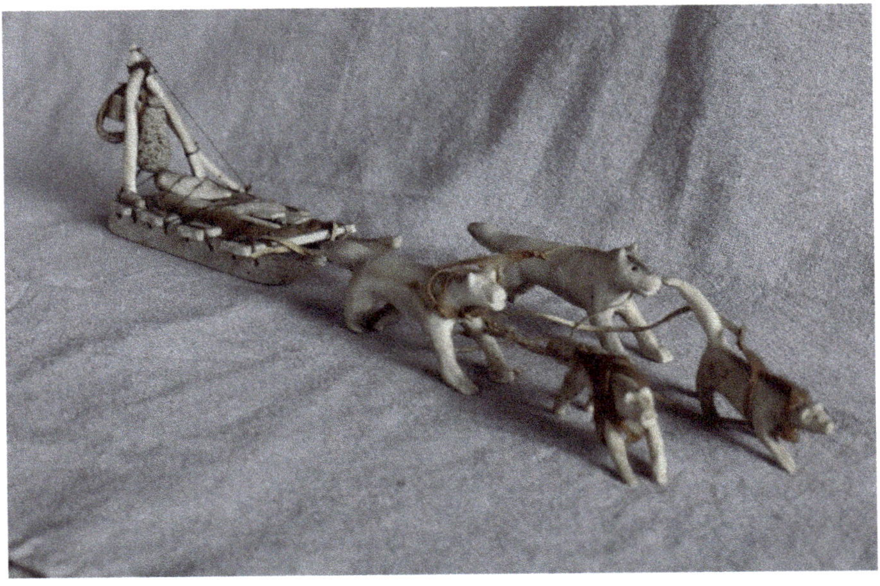

11 coming home

School had closed for the year, and we were waiting to be air-lifted out. Time hung heavy on our hands. Here is the letter I wrote after we had reached Ottawa when I was staying with Mr and Mrs Mac.

July 21st

Beacon Arms Hotel, Ottawa, that's where we spent the first night after we landed. All on the Government. Now, I sit beside the Ottawa river at Mr and Mrs Mac's cottage, at Black Bay, having a much-needed quiet time and catching up on letters. Mrs Mac looks after me—I am spoilt. Well, to go back a long way, it all seems very remote now. With all the things at school to finish off and pack, it was an agony trying to get through each day. School finished on 27th June, and then began an endurance test of waiting for the ice to break up, so we could leave. One of the women put on a tea for us, and the rest of the settlement also put on a surprise party. They had made posters for each of us, all very hilarious.

The rain came and rained for days; the mud drove us mad. After the first few days, I was ready to go. Daylight was with us for nearly 24 hours, and trying to sleep with kids running past the house on their way up the fjord, was a challenge. It wasn't until the 10th July that the ice broke up and went out. It didn't do us much good as we still had to wait for a plane to come in.

A highlight of this time was when Doug, the Development Officer, suggested we have a trip out to Cumberland Sound on the Longliner, to go fishing for Arctic char. We left early in the morning and spent the day fishing and clambering over the rocks. Everyone began to pull in fish; they almost leapt onto the lines. A line was thrust into my hands, and I cast it out. No fish. They were swimming all around, but not taking my bait. I think it might have something to do with the fact that my sympathies are with the fish. I have yet to catch a fish. Coming back that night, we ran into one of the worst storms of the year. The boat was pitching all over. We made it back soaked and glad to be on land. I spent the rest of the night wondering if my roof would blow off, or if the boys were at the bottom of the fjord. We found out later, that there had been 100-mile-an-hour gusts that night.

Monday, we heard there was a plane in Frobisher Bay. A Corsair finally came Tuesday at midday and landed in the fjord; we were on our way. All of the community was lined up along the shore watching us leave. As I was scrambling into the canoe, I heard,

"Ulisai, you come back!"

"No," I replied.

"Aieee!" went up the wail.

It wasn't until I left that I knew I had been accepted; a very bittersweet moment for me. I was nearly sick with worry about how I was going to manage when we arrived 'outside'. One becomes set in a pattern of life. It is very difficult to imagine any other.

We made Frobisher Bay in time for afternoon tea, and spent the next thirty hours there, waiting for a plane to pick us up. I was taken out that night, had a really good time, and received more invitations than I could possibly accept! Nordair finally left at 9pm, and we travelled until 2am. It was a long, long journey. All of us were tired and really wrought up.

For a few weeks, we had had almost no night. Seeing Montreal at last, all lit up, was our first experience of darkness for a long time. It was 4am before we were settled in the Montreal Hilton, a very plush hotel with swimming pool. No swim for us, too lily-white. Smithy and I shared a room.

Next morning up and out shopping for much-needed clothes. The humidity was up in the 80s. We had left Pang about 10 degrees above. I did not need my parka here. We used every air-conditioned place we could find.

At the Montreal airport, we teachers sadly said our goodbyes to each other. After spending the past year together, we were all going our different ways. I caught a flight to Ottawa and booked into the Beacon Arms Hotel. I then went to the Department of Education to sign off. They offered me a position on Broughton Island, but I turned it down. I didn't want to go back to the Eastern Arctic. If it had been the Western Arctic, I might have taken it. There are different challenges, but more trees, animals and people!

Mr and Mrs Mac picked me up and brought me up to the bach. Twelve months without speed made my senses reject fast movement, and I had to physically move myself to the centre of the seat. I had an almost uncontrollable urge to open the door and jump out. This feeling did not go away for many months.

At the bach, peace and quiet gave me time to recuperate. Two fiddles and a guitar the next night provided a very entertaining evening. Just what I needed.

On our return to Ottawa, I rang Jean, then caught a flight from Ottawa to Toronto to Calgary, first-class with all the trimmings. Then to Lethbridge. Big excitement as Jean and Howard were there to pick me up, new car and all. Home to Vauxhall. Being home was all I had imagined. Jean said I could have my old room for free for as long as I wanted. I was overwhelmed. Kenny was the biggest shock; he was

> talking like a book.
>
> They had a ticket for the Legion BBQ. I didn't realise I knew so many people. It's just like I'd never been away. It's about 88 degrees outside at the moment, and I'm waiting for Howard to come. We are off to pick up hay bales, good farming stuff. The local fair came up while I was there, and we decided to put our talents to the test. Jean was a superb baker. I added my skills to the mix, and we entered many of the classes. I duly wrote out the entry forms. The results came back: "This is too much like your friend's." Oops.

I had booked myself a trip down the American West through Mexico and back to Los Angeles, before flying home. All too soon, the time came to leave again. It was very difficult saying goodbye to the kids; many tears were shed. Howard, Jean and Lillian (Jean's sister), came to the bus station to see me off.

Unbeknownst to me, my departure was reported on TV—a great spiel about my adventures and a picture of me walking in a marathon. World-famous in Vauxhall!

> Wednesday, I slipped out of town and had an enjoyable trip to Great Falls, Montana. The bus driver was a wit. I was to discover my travel agent had not booked any of my accommodation. I was met with blank stares when I came to the hotels on the list. Fortunately, I was able to get into each one. I spent the night in Great Falls avoiding a misunderstood man, "My wife doesn't understand me.

The next day, I caught a 2.30pm plane to Denver; it leapt about in the sky over the mountains around Cheyenne. I was not a well girl. Found my hotel, booked in, and wandered around this quaint western town set in the mountains.

On the following day, I had a good flight to El Paso. The country is vast and barren, and the only apparent settlements are along rivers. Landing in El Paso, I made my way to my hotel for the night, right in the middle of town. I was able to go out the front door, into the shopping centre. The Rio Grande river flows between El Paso and Juarez, the twin city in Mexico. The shops there are open until two in the morning. Feeling apprehensive about it all, I went on a tour and ate and drank my way around Juarez. I joined up with a New York stockbroker for the tour, and we had loads of fun. I bought a leather handbag with money which Jean had supplied me to buy myself one as a present from her. It was my bag for many years.

On the following day, I went on a bus tour inland to the Carlsbad Caverns in New Mexico. The land was covered with arid sagebrush, and it was hot. For this trip, I teamed up with a stockbroker from Holland. We enjoyed our day, and at the end of it, he went north, and I went south. The caverns are a vast network 600 feet underground, with stalagmites and stalactites of grand proportions—a stunning sight.

In the morning, I headed out for Juarez with a sinking feeling in my stomach and everyone's warnings ringing in my ears. I passed through Customs and went to buy my ticket for Mexico City. The bus driver took pity on me and put me on a bus. I thought he said it took 24 hours, but I was wrong. This bus went the LONG way round.

After catching up on sleep, I realized with horror that I might starve. I didn't know enough Mexican (Spanish) to ask for food and drink. Eventually, some vendors came on board, and I plucked up courage and bought a bottle of pop. It was nectar to me. The lady in front of me conversed in broken English. She wrote it a lot better, so we communicated that way. There had been a rather grubby, unsavoury man who kept pestering me. She wrote, "I do not like that man." I wrote back, "No, I don't either." Fortunately, he got off, and I was very relieved.

We went up in the mountains and along the way, and ran into a storm. The water was up around the wheels of the bus. Scary. The scenery along the way was truly amazing. In the north, there were vast areas of cactus, and the further south we came, the scenery gradually changed into cultivated areas where farmers existed as they had for hundreds of years. Their adobe houses and few animals were much as you would expect.

As we continued on, we found large cultivated areas, mostly government-owned. Towns came and went, but I was too tired to take much notice. We arrived in Mexico City at 10 o'clock at night.

I had to find my hotel. A taxi ride later, we were there, only to find there was no reservation, again. They managed to conjure up a room, so all was saved. Shower, meal and clean clothes were bliss, and I tumbled into bed and slept.

In the morning, I was woken by the sound of marching feet. "You've done it now, Bev. The middle of a revolution, and nobody knows where you are." Yes, there were troops out there. I was terrified. Phew, it turned out to be Independence Day celebrations. A huge parade at 11am was very spectacular.

The Cathedral in Mexico City

This was 1968, and the Olympic Games were on. I went on a tour of the Olympic Village, and I ran into the New Zealand rowing team. Kiwi voices, Hurrah! I don't think they shared my enthusiasm at the meeting.

Mexico City has pyramids, and I went on an evening tour to see them. How fortunate that there was a practice going on for the opening of the games, one of those special times you never forget.

I was crossing over to Acapulco, and a large gentleman in flash clothes and a very large car with driver offered to take me. Yes, I took up the offer. I did not feel good about the whole adventure, so I transferred to a bus when we reached Taxco. Taxco is built on silver; the Spaniards mined silver there. The town sits on the side of the mountain, with narrow cobbled streets. It's totally charming. The whole town is a museum. You cannot change anything without permission, so it truly feels like a time warp.

Acapulco—the mecca of so many of my dreams. My hotel room was dirty, and it smelled—not a good beginning. The next day, I was out shopping. I had a towel jacket made for the beach, which was most useful and which I still have today. A night-time harbour cruise showed the whole area in all its beauty. With my new beach towel, under an umbrella, drinking coco locos, life couldn't be better.

A Street scene in Taxco

All too soon, I was on my way to Los Angeles. From there, the flight home to New Zealand beckoned, and I was ready to go. Thirteen hours later, I touched down in Auckland. Mum and Johnny were there to welcome me home.

epilogue

The trip home to New Plymouth, passed in a blur of fatigue and chatter. Once home, an endless stream of visitors kept the kettle boiling and the chat going. Photos and artefacts were admired and exclaimed over.

My most pressing need was money. I had spent every penny I'd earned and now needed a job. I managed to get a short-term teaching position at Woodstock School in Hamilton.

I was soon on my way again, to stay with Cousin Joy and her family. Relief.

Such was the interest in my exploits that I was called upon to show slides and tell people of my adventures. Baffin Island remained a complete mystery to them.

Jean & Howard in front of their house (2000)

My Canadian family remained in my life with letters regularly exchanged.

In 2000, we went to Canada to introduce my husband, Peter, to my families there.

Pangnirtung could not expand beyond the limited land available. The all-weather airstrip, which was completed the following year, made outside contact with the world much more readily available. It has become a launching place for trips to the Auyuittuq National Park and Kekerten Territorial Park.

Marilyn and Chuck Mears on our trip in 2000

It is worthwhile to look up Pangnirtung on the Internet and find the many adventures that are available today for the Intrepid Traveller. As well as the national parks nearby to explore, there is fishing, hunting and camping. The settlement has a thriving arts and crafts industry available. Remember it is cold all year round, so the northern summertime, from June to August, is the better time to visit.

Teacher returns from the Arctic

Teaching Eskimo children to speak English in a remote settlement in Arctic Canada has been the task for the past year of Miss Beverly Andrews, a former teacher at Te Uku School.

Miss Andrews, who has just returned from Pangnirtung, an isolated settlement on Baffin Island in the Canadian Eastern Arctic, said she found it hard to break down the children's natural reserve and shyness.

"Just when I thought I had won them over, they would withdraw into their shells again," she said.

☆

Miss Andrews was one of 30 white people living at the settlement. They were either employed by the Hudson Bay Company, the Royal Canadian Mounted Police or a chain of radar stations. Frobishar Bay, the nearest town of any size, was 250 miles away.

Communication with the outside world was by radio telephone. Mail arrived fortnightly by small ski or float planes.

Miss Andrews said the longest lapse between mails came during the Arctic winter when the mail was delayed for two-and-a-half months. It finally arrived a week before Christmas, just when the Pangnirtung residents had given up hope of receiving it in time for Christmas.

☆

During the summer, when the fiord was free of ice, bulk supplies of food, enough to last a year, were ordered, as air freighting was expensive during the winter.

Miss Andrews said that nearly everything she ate, came out of a can. Salad and fresh fruit, occasionally flown in especially from Montreal, were considered a treat.

Principal source of income for the Eskimos living in the area came from carving caribou horn, soapstone or whalebone. Supplies of whalebone, according to Miss Andrews, are becoming scarce and whalebone carvings are expected to become comparatively rare and priceless.

☆

Miss Andrews said that many of the men employed in the Arctic had sought refuge there from domestic troubles or for other personal reasons. For most of them, the Arctic had a compelling effect, which prompted them to stay.

After about a year in New Zealand, Miss Andrews said that she may also return to the Arctic.

MISS BEVERLEY ANDREWS, wearing a parka made for her by an Eskimo friend. A former Te Uku School teacher, Miss Andrews corresponded regularly with Waikato people during the time she was in Arctic Canada, and stories of her year among the Eskimos have appeared in The Times previously. Mail from home, according to her, was the only way to fight the hopeless feeling that comes from extreme isolation.

Glossary

KAMIK: an outer boot made of sealskin. The *kamik* was used in the Eastern Arctic. It was constructed with a round pattern for men, and an up and down pattern for women. The colour contrast to make the pattern was achieved with soaking the sealskin in urine.

KAYAK: One or two-person canoe.

KOMATIK: sled pulled by dogs.

KUDLI: A cooking and heating vessel made of hollowed-out soapstone. This was used before the introduction of modern cooking utensils.

MUKLUK: An outer boot from the Western Arctic. This was shorter than the Kamik and made from other materials, such as horsehide, or caribou but with colourful markings.

MUKTUK: whale blubber chewed like chewing gum.

OOKPIC: snow owl.

PANGNIRTUNG: Place of the bull caribou, also nicknamed the Switzerland of the Arctic.

SKI-DOO: Ski-Doo is a brand name of snowmobile manufactured by Bombardier Recreational Products and introduced in 1959.

TUKTUK: Caribou

ULU: All-purpose half circle steel knife with an upward wooden handle used for cutting, skinning, and scraping.

arger canoe used for transporting larger materials.

about bev

Bev Bevan (nee Andrews) taught for many years after returning to New Zealand. Travelling adventures continued and Bev met her husband, Peter, on a bus tour around Australia in 1969. Just recently, in 2020, they celebrated their 50th wedding anniversary. They live in Tamahere, just south of Hamilton, New Zealand, and have two children and three grandchildren. The whole family continue to travel and explore.